The Stress
Management Handbook

Lori A. Leyden-Rubenstein, Ph.D.
Foreword by Stephen T. Sinatra, M.D.

The Stress Management Handbook

Strategies for Health and Inner Peace

KEATS PUBLISHING, INC.
NEW CANAAN, CONNECTICUT

The Stress Management Handbook is not intended as medical advice. Its intent is solely informational and educational. Please consult a health professional should the need for one be indicated.

THE STRESS MANAGEMENT HANDBOOK

Copyright © 1998 by Lori A. Leyden-Rubenstein

Library of Congress Cataloging-in-Publication Data

Leyden-Rubenstein, Lori A.
    The stress management handbook : strategies for health and inner peace / Lori A. Leyden-Rubenstein : forward by Stephen T. Sinatra.
        p.   cm.
    Includes bibliographical references and index.
    ISBN: 0-87983-794-2
    1. Stress (Psychology)   2. Stress management   I. Title.
BF675.S75L49   1998
155.9'042—dc21   97-39243
                                                                            CIP

Printed in the United States of America

Keats Publishing, Inc.
27 Pine Street (Box 876)
New Canaan, Connecticut 06840-0876
Website Address: www.keats.com

To my precious husband Howard Rubenstein,
who has created a special womb for me to grow in.
The richness of our sacred partnership
continues to amaze and inspire me.

Contents

9
Stress, Spirituality and Inner Peace 87

10
Do It Now! Strategies for Relieving Stress 92

Foreword

The word "stress" is used so often these days that it has become a moniker of sorts for the age in which we live. In the years to come, ours may well be viewed not so much as "The High-tech Age," but "The Stress Age." In fact, stress has spawned its own industry, one rife with quick-fix cure-alls and personality quizzes that promise us a better quality of life in no time at all—and with very little effort on our part.

I wish it were so easy. While stress can be a time bomb, manifesting itself in a host of illnesses, those most in need of help will not find it by taking a pop magazine quiz. In fact, the reality of the grip that stress has on their lives and their health usually isn't apparent until they end up in a doctor's office seeking treatment for anything from rashes and headaches to heart disease and cancer.

Surveys indicate that stress today accounts for about 80 percent of all visits to doctors' offices. While this figure may be relatively new, the premise certainly is not. For centuries, we have known of the role that psychosocial and behavioral factors play in disease. Hippocrates and Maimonides both concluded that "emotional disturbances cause marked changes in the body."

While stress has always been a factor in disease, it appears to be an even greater one now. We can attribute this to the 20th century—a high-tech society poised to compete on demand—one where business is highly structured and ultrademanding and where the words "leisure time" no longer accurately describe how we spend our spare time. Our leisure activities are both active and very often competitive. Little time, if any, is devoted to relaxation or even to casual conversation. Our motto has become "work hard, play hard."

We are also a society that rewards left-brain activities like analysis, counting, scheduling and planning. Intuition and creativity, which stem from our right brain, are perceived as having less value.

Indeed, there can no longer be any doubt about the relationship between stress and disease. As a cardiologist who treats patients struggling with heart illness every day, I am always impressed by the way in which our underlying emotions, often masked by stress, can inhibit our ability to heal ourselves.

Although many diseases still have congenital, nutritional and infectious origins, the majority of diseases of the 21st century will result from smoking, excessive drinking and other damaging lifestyle habits. Men's and women's inability to adapt to stress is a major contributor to disease. Because of this, both physician and patient must be aware of—and fully explore—how the patient's personality and reaction to life experiences has created a lifetime of stress leading to illness and disease.

It is one of the biggest challenges the medical profession faces. As healers, we must be prepared to convey this message: stress doesn't cause damage, it's how we react to stress over time that causes the damage. It is critical therefore to assess the pivotal role that personality and behavioral traits play in determining illness, especially cancer and cardiovascular disease.

We already know, for instance, that people with fear, resentment, suppressed anger, depression and despair get sick more often and have a significantly higher incidence of disease when compared to those with a positive outlook on life.

If we can contribute, however unwittingly, to our own illness, we can also utilize the power of the mind to heal the body and keep it healthy. And harnessed properly, the emotions and reactions that hurt our bodies also can heal them.

The trick is to find the silver lining in the negative cloud. We can start by learning to laugh at ourselves and to take things less seriously; by refusing to internalize personal or work pressures, by reaching out and loving ourselves and others and, in return, accepting the affection others give us. Opening our hearts to love and forgiving creates positive forces and emotions that heal.

As we hurtle toward the next century, it behooves all health professionals to explore the underlying causes that contribute to disease and to help their patients recognize and alter their behavior. We must step beyond the initial diagnosis and treatment protocol and actively deal with the underlying cause of each patient's illness.

Although we cannot remove patients' stress, past or present, we can teach them how to alter and control stress by exploring the negative forces, feelings, attitudes and beliefs, as well as the destructive personality traits that have long contributed to illness in our society. In that way, the practitioner and the patient become partners in the treatment and control of disease. Only then can health truly be affected and well-being maintained.

In this exceptional book, Lori Leyden-Rubenstein gives you powerful tools to help you deal effectively with stress. *The Stress Management Handbook* offers practical and potent solutions to stress that will help you reclaim your life. Dr. Leyden-Rubenstein gives readers the chance to empower themselves by taking an active role in their own healing. Health professionals will also find this book to be a valuable resource guide for treating patients with stress-related symptoms and illnesses.

STEPHEN T. SINATRA, M.D.

Acknowledgements

I am deeply grateful for having met these people on my spiritual path:

○ Darlene Trew Crist whose editorial expertise and generosity of spirit contributed to the quality of this work.

○ Dr. George Burnell whose openness to holistic approaches provided a perfect blend of guidance and encouragement when this work was the focus of my dissertation.

○ Susan Fox and Barbara Ganim whose caring friendships and shared professional interests helped me find my life's work.

○ Virginia Chapin whose professional nurturing provided me with the safety to begin my emotional healing in earnest.

○ Skip Walsh and Maggie Adair-Coggeshall whose unconditional acceptance and love helped me to begin to love myself.

○ Frank Matune who encouraged me to honor myself and my spiritual search.

○ Phyllis Herman and everyone at Keats Publishing who believed in my work.

○ Joan Borysenko, Jon Kabat-Zinn, Herbert Benson, Bernie Siegel, Peter Breggin, Ty Colbert, Dick Olney, F. Scott Peck,

Wayne Muller, Nathaniel Branden, Charles Whitfield, John Bradshaw, Deepak Chopra, Gary Zukav, Susan Forward, Dawn Eagle Woman, Martin Hart and others whose work has inspired me and guided me on my healing journey.

○ Marilyn Van Derbur Atler and Frank Fitzpatrick whose courage and perseverance moved me to begin to release the shame of childhood sexual abuse and whose voices have reminded us to protect and believe our children.

○ Lazaris whose wisdom and guidance has taught me to overcome struggle and to live joyfully, in gratitude and wonder.

○ My clients whose trust in me has profoundly contributed to my own personal healing and deep sense of connection with others. I feel a strong sense of honor for, and commitment to those of you who have allowed me to share in your healing journey in some way.

Introduction

I could easily blame stress for the many emotional and physical symptoms I experienced from early childhood. Free-floating anxiety, feeling unworthy and undeserving of love and happiness, feeling hypersensitive and yet numb to many of my emotions and constantly judging, criticizing and berating myself were just some of the unhealthy defense mechanisms I had learned over the years to cope with stress. Because I now know how intimately interrelated the mind and the body are, I believe these defense mechanisms, as well as others, played a significant role in creating the many physical symptoms I experienced over the years, including gastrointestinal problems, headaches, insomnia, chronic back pain, endometriosis, psoriasis and TMJ (Temporomandibular Joint Disorder—a jaw dysfunction that results in head and neck pain).

Simply blaming stress, however, wasn't enough. It took landing in the hospital to motivate me to learn ways I could alleviate stress and participate in my own emotional and physical healing. For me, the true beginning was accepting responsibility for myself and risking new behaviors. Clearly, the old ones weren't working.

The impetus for this book came from my own experience of healing from stress-related thoughts, emotions and illnesses as well as finding my life's work. It deeply reflects my approach to my own life and to my work as a psychotherapist. The book is meant to be a "how-to" stress and anxiety management guide for individuals as well as health care and mental health care professionals. It's based on the latest scientific evidence showing that a mind/body/spirit approach is a valid and effective way to manage stress and anxiety. I've included over 50 practical strategies—strategies that I've developed and that I use myself—to relieve stress and feel a sense of inner peace.

Why Read Another Self-help Book?

If you're at a point where you can honestly admit that you're not doing anything to cope with your stress in a healthy way, or if your current strategies just aren't working well enough for you to see positive results, this book may provide you with the information and incentive you need to manage your stress and find a sense of inner peace.

If you're on psychiatric medication for stress and/or anxiety, if it's been suggested to you as a treatment strategy and you are reluctant to take drugs, if you are unaware of the dangers and side effects of these medications, then you owe it to yourself to ask questions and explore other options. Ask your physician, psychiatrist or counselor what he or she knows about the mind/body connection as it relates to stress. Ask them what they know or can teach you about non-drug mind/body strategies to alleviate stress. If you aren't satisfied with the response, read this book.

The best time to read this book is *before* you feel stressed or develop a stress-related illness. Psychologist and self-help guru Wayne Dyer, author of *Your Sacred Self*, has often said, "You don't have to be sick to get better!" Many people wait until an emotional or physical crisis hits them before they become "teachable." That is, they lack the motivation to manage their stress until something bad happens. The moments we need stress management strategies the most are usually the moments when we're least able to use them—unless those strategies are already an integral part of our behavior.

I've read a lot of self-help and psychology books over the years. I've spent over 20 years studying psychotherapy and participating in many kinds of psychotherapy and personal and spiritual growth workshops. But it wasn't until I committed myself to putting that knowledge into action and practicing the techniques I learned and developed, that I actually saw positive changes take effect. My hope is that by reading this book you will feel motivated and empowered to make positive changes in your life and learn to participate in your own physical and emotional healing—starting now. More important, I hope that this book can be your personal road map to finding the sense of inner peace that I am so grateful to have in my life.

My Approach

Even though scientific evidence supports mind/body/spirit approaches as more effective than traditional medical or psychological approaches for dealing with stress and healing from stress-related illnesses, most doctors and therapists don't know how to use them. If you go to your doctor with concerns about feeling anxious, panicky, stressed or depressed, he or she is usually only trained to provide comfort with medication. Many psychotherapists and counselors are trained to support the medication approach with traditional talk therapy. The problem is, psychiatric medication and talk therapy *without an effective stress management program* do not cure stress-related symptoms and problems. For the most part, they merely provide superficial stop-gap measures.

The underlying assumption of my mind/body/spirit approach is that negative thoughts and beliefs about our ability to cope with what life presents us trigger a physiological reaction in the body called the stress response. In other words, we experience stress when we tell ourselves that we are being threatened in some way and we may not be able to cope with that threat.

If the stress response is triggered often enough without healthy intervention, it will affect our health and well-being.

If thoughts, particularly thoughts about ourselves, are at the core of our experience of stress, then we need to be aware of what we are telling ourselves about ourselves. I believe that people who feel stressed or anxious are telling themselves negative things about themselves and, as a result, feel threatened by the circumstances, events, conditions or people they encounter. Each of us experiences our own unique set of stressors. But it's not the stressors themselves that create the stress experience in us; rather, it's how we perceive those stressors and how we've learned to react to them.

We are our own biggest source of stress because of what we tell ourselves about ourselves and about the situation we find ourselves in.

Most people who are stressed or anxious are telling themselves that they are trapped in some way. They often have the false belief that there are no options. In this emotional state they are either unable to consider what options are available to them or they are unwilling to do so because the options may appear inconvenient, troublesome or even impossible. This tends to impair their confidence that they can cope effectively with whatever threat they are perceiving. We know that the vast majority of our negative thoughts are distortions of reality. In fact, there are always options, even if the only option available to us is to change our perception of the situation by viewing it differently.

Have you ever felt trapped in a job you didn't like and told yourself you had no choice but to stay in the job—because of the money, because it was just too difficult to look for another job, because it wouldn't look good on your resume, or because you didn't know what else you wanted to do? But did you really consider all the choices you had available to you? For instance, you could choose to try to do something about the things you don't like about the job—ask for a transfer, try to improve relationships with difficult people, develop a new approach to disagreeable tasks. If that doesn't work, you really do have the choice to quit. You may not like the consequences of having to ask family members for help, dipping into your savings to tide you over, going on unemployment or welfare, but quitting is an option. You have a choice to take another kind of job, one that's less stressful, while you figure out what to do next. You always have the choice to find another job—even if it pays less money or requires you to perform tasks that you may consider yourself overqualified for.

You could become self-employed or start your own business. Even though this option opens concerns about benefits and added responsibilities, among other things, it is a choice. You have the choice to research what options are open to you. You could begin by talking to a job counselor, reading the classifieds, or talking to people at other companies to find out about job openings. You also have the option to change your perception of being trapped in the job. You could choose to stay in the job because it provides you with a good salary, security and/or the prestige you desire. In other words, you have the choice to take responsibility for why you stay in the job as opposed to focusing on everything that's wrong with it. You could choose to see things differently. Maybe your boss isn't out to get you, maybe he just has problems of his own that have nothing to do with you. Maybe those policies and procedures that are annoying and inconvenient to you really are for the good of the company as a whole.

I could go on, but you probably get the point. The experience of stress can block us from considering all our options. When we don't consider all our options, we are less able to take responsibility for ourselves, less able to make conscious choices from a place of freedom and less able to empower ourselves. And this is one of the reasons it is so important for us to be aware of what we are telling ourselves about ourselves and our ability to cope with the situation we are in.

When we feel stressed, angry, anxious, fearful, depressed or any combination of these feelings, we have the tendency to stay stuck there, focusing on our negative thoughts and emotions about the person or situation that we blame for causing our stress. Then we spend an inordinate amount of time rehashing, analyzing, judging or feeling like a victim. This kind of reaction saps our energy and eliminates our healthy sense of control and personal power—not to mention the physical effect it has on our bodies.

To many people, fear, anger and sadness are bad, and the current medical philosophy often supports medicating those feelings. But we need to recognize that feelings are really very powerful tools that tell us whether or not our needs are being met. They help us to negotiate our world. Real personal power lies in reflecting on our thoughts, feelings and needs and then doing something constructive to resolve them in a healthy way.

Managing our stress and participating in our own healing goes beyond attending to this thought-feel-need relationship, however. It extends to learning to listen to our body and our inner voice. I believe that we were all born with the inherent capacity to know, at every given moment in time, exactly what we need and what is best for us. This sense of knowing comes from a calm, peaceful place inside of us where we can access all that we need to know to make decisions for ourselves. When we allow ourselves to move into this quiet space within, we are able to listen to what is variously called our "inner voice," "inner wisdom" or "higher self."

The problem is that many of us have lost touch with our inner voice by focusing on "shoulds" and other people's opinions and expectations. We need to reclaim that skill. Our bodies and our minds are linked by a complex system of neurological and physiological connections. As a result, when we learn to tune in to our mind/body connection we can tune in to the unique knowledge it has to offer us about ourselves. By doing so, we can learn to feel the safety that comes from knowing that while we can't control everything that happens to us, we can control how we react by going within to find out what we need to do to take care of ourselves.

Because we experience stress when we tell ourselves that we are being threatened in some way, managing stress and maintaining inner peace depends a great deal on developing a sense of internal safety. If we have low self-esteem, feel inadequate, and/or beat ourselves up mentally with negative self-talk, our sense of internal safety is constantly being compromised.

On a personal level then, it becomes important for us to examine our thoughts and beliefs about ourselves, how we talk to ourselves, and where we are in terms of our self-esteem and self-worth. From a spiritual perspective what this really means is that we need to look at our relationship with ourselves. We need to ask ourselves questions like: "How much do I honor and respect myself?" and, "To what extent do I love myself and treat myself with unconditional acceptance and compassion?"

If you feel stressed or anxious, you probably don't have a strong sense of internal safety and chances are you'll also find that your relationship with yourself is not a very positive one.

This is why my work focuses on helping people to discover their own personal strength—giving them practical mind/body/ spirit strategies to deal with and overcome the emotional and physical challenges they experience in their daily lives.

On a basic level, it's about teaching people how to feel good about themselves, to learn to see options and to develop healthy coping skills. On a spiritual level, it's about teaching people to feel the safety that comes from listening to their inner voice or higher self, to feel self-love and inner validation, to find meaning in life, and to feel connected to others and a Divine power by practicing compassion, gratitude and wonder. I find that inner peace flows naturally from engaging in these strategies. As we nurture these qualities in ourselves, we find it easier to release the stress and fear that come with feeling threatened. It also becomes easier to view stressors as opportunities for growth and to trust in our ability to successfully negotiate the circumstances of our lives.

I fully recognize that people's lives are complicated and that their stress and emotional woundedness can be very deep. At first glance, studying my approach and practicing the strategies outlined in this book may seem too simple. Once you have committed to using them, however, you will understand that there are many levels to managing your stress and many opportunities for growth. This handbook is meant to provide you with a baseline of mental, emotional, physical and spiritual support. It is also meant to be a springboard from which you can develop a sense of internal safety to cope more effectively with the stress in your life.

Remember . . .
*There are **powerful tools available to help you**,*
*and you have the **personal power to use them**.*

Special note to readers

The scientific information presented in this work is only a representative sample of relevant research pertaining to stress management and the mind/body connection. The complexities of the mind/body/spirit connection are not yet fully understood. The stress management approach described here is based on scientific information currently available and on my own clinical and personal experience.

The strategies and information found in this book are not intended as a replacement for appropriate medical or mental health treatment. Rather, they are meant to be used as a significant complement to traditional treatment.

Note to mental health care professionals

The holistic stress management approach described here is not meant to be applied as a cookbook of strategies. Rather, it is most important that these techniques be used and recommended by professionals who have tested them, incorporated them into their own lives, and realized the benefits of holistic stress management for themselves. This is not a comprehensive guide for the practice of psychotherapy. It is expected that professionals will evaluate this material and integrate it into their own work, as appropriate, based on their own training and experience.

Why Bother?

"Why bother?" many people say, "I don't have control over the things that create stress for me (my demanding boss, escalating expenses, sick mother) and, anyway, things will never change." Well, certain things may not change and you don't necessarily have control over everything that happens to you. But you *do* have control over one very important thing: you have control over changing yourself. And there are some very compelling reasons to motivate you to change.

According to well-known stress researcher Kenneth Pelletier, author of *Mind as Healer, Mind as Slayer*:

o Between 80 and 90 percent of all illness is stress-related. (Other researchers believe that all illness—at least in part—is stress-related.)
o Nearly 100 million Americans suffer from stress-related illness.
o Between 75 and 90 percent of all visits to the doctor are for stress and anxiety-related concerns.

Not only do we suffer from the physical effects of stress, we are *dying* because of it. Consider this:

o Stress is linked to the six leading causes of death—heart disease, cancer, lung disease, accidents, cirrhosis of the liver
  and suicide.

If you've experienced any of these serious conditions or even
if you've been to the doctor recently, think about how stress has
affected you. Then think about doing something about it!

If you're lucky enough to have escaped stress-related illness,
think about the impact stress may be having on your emotional
health. Millions of people suffer emotional challenges because of
stress related to:

o job
o family
o financial pressures
o relationships
o addictions
o guilt
o self-esteem
o life changes
o emotional, physical or sexual trauma

Not only does stress cost us in terms of our emotional and
physical health, it also affects us economically and financially.
The Department of Health and Human Services tells us that
stress costs American industry more than $300 billion each year
in absenteeism, reduced productivity and workers' compensation
benefits. That's $7,500 for each employee every year. Of course,
ultimately, we all bear this cost because it gets passed on to us
in the form of increased prices for goods and services.

So, "why bother?" Think about the following phrase for a
moment:

*If you always do what you've always done, you'll always get
what you've always gotten.*

In other words, if your present attempts to manage your
stress aren't working as effectively for you as you would like, it's

time to take responsibility for yourself and risk some new behaviors. If your health, well-being and financial security are important to you then you have enough compelling reasons to learn to manage your stress in new, healthy ways.

My Stress Story

I was an anxious, hyper-vigilant child. As a four-year-old, I remember feeling alone and different from others, somehow flawed and not good enough. Typical of a firstborn, I was also serious and compliant, as well as being a perfectionist and an over-achiever. I worried about being a "good girl," not making mistakes, being at the top of my class, pleasing others, and having everyone like me. By the time I was ten, I had persistent headaches and stomachaches and was unable to sleep for hours after going to bed.

My life as a 12-year-old intensified and deepened those feelings. One of the things that happened that year was that I lost the person I was closest to—my mother's mother—my "Nanna." She lived across town but would come over after work to baby-sit for us when Mom and Dad were working or out for the evening.

Nanna was in the hospital for several long summer months before her death. It was a frightening time for me not only because I couldn't spend time with her but because of a certain superstition that heavily influenced my family. Before she went into the hospital I would hear Nanna and my mother talking about an old Irish belief that "God gives one new life to a family for one old life." My mother was pregnant and due to give birth within months. Nanna was really worried because she fervently believed that, if she had the operation she needed, she would be the "old life" that was taken in order for the "new life" to be born. Nanna did have her operation that summer. In the meantime, I took on her duty of baby-sitting for my three siblings, aged ten, eight and three, while Mom visited her daily in the hospital. My sister was born in August and the superstition was fulfilled—my grandmother died very shortly after her birth. I was devastated when I lost her. Nanna was my confidante and my source of unconditional love. I was also frightened of a God who could be so vengeful.

At the same time I felt tense and anxious about baby-sitting for three children and an infant when my parents were working or out for the evening. I felt frustrated and overwhelmed when my rambunctious brother and two sisters acted up or fought with each other. I was either yelling at them or crying because I didn't know what to do to get them to stop. I was always fearful that they would wake up the baby. One of my sisters used to have episodes where she would get up out of bed and run around the house crying and in fear of something—all while she was in a deep sleep. These incidents really scared me because I didn't understand what was happening to her. Since I couldn't get her to wake up, I'd just have to wait it out until I could guide her back to bed. Caring for an infant made me feel even more inadequate. Although I took my job as caretaker very seriously, I rarely felt comfortable with what I was doing. I remember being nervous about getting in trouble for using adhesive tape to keep my sister's cloth diapers closed because I was afraid to stick her with the safety pin. Imagine my surprise some 20 years later when diapers were sold with the tape already in place—I could have made millions!

From the time I made my First Communion at age seven, I took my religious beliefs very seriously. As an Irish Catholic attending parochial school, I followed rules like not eating meat on Friday, going to church every Sunday, and making sacrifices for Lent. It was not unusual for me to go to daily mass before school and spend extra time in church praying. I remember having a strong desire to be "holy" in God's eyes. That September after Nanna died, a new priest was transferred to our parish. He organized religious and social activities just for kids and put together a special group of seventh and eighth grade guitarists and singers for folk masses on Sundays. I was thrilled when he chose me to be one of the only seventh grade singers included in his special group. He even taught me to play the guitar so I could play in the folk masses.

I believed with all my heart that I was as close to God as any child could be—until this 30-year-old man I revered (my parish priest, "God's representative on earth") started to sexually abuse me. I trusted this person so completely that I did not question what he was doing to me. Being so young and entirely naive, I had no way of associating what he was doing to me with sex. I felt like I was being lulled into some kind of trance, watching what was happening from somewhere outside myself. All I knew was that I felt sick all the time, my sleeping problems got worse, my stomach was in knots, and I was completely terrified, especially the many times he would arrange to meet me before school in secret places in the church. I thought I was safe once I was in school but then he convinced the principal to send me over to the rectory during the day for one reason or another and my sense of helplessness skyrocketed. After many months, he told me that he had confessed his "sins with me" to another priest in the parish. I will never forget the blinding, weight-crushing, fear and shame that filled my body as I took on the burden of believing that I had sinned too. And I believed my sin was worse. Since I had been taught that priests were infallible, my child's mind fervently believed that it was all my fault, that I was responsible for making this man break his vows to God, and that there was something terribly wrong with me. I desperately tried to stay away from him, but he was cunning in arranging circumstances to be near me. He started to stalk me, calling my house and hanging up until I answered the phone, finding reasons to visit my home. He would sit in his car outside my house for hours while my parents were out and I was baby-sitting. Once he tried to get in the house after my brother and sisters had gone to bed. I ran around the house frantically locking all the doors and windows.

I spent many years waiting for God to punish me, believing as I had been taught, that "only through pain and suffering could I hope to cleanse my soul of my wicked sins." As a 12-year-old, I was painfully ashamed and petrified to tell anyone. I felt completely alone with my fear, my shame and my distorted beliefs. The emotional, physical and spiritual scars of this particular wound left me numb and traumatized. More than 20 years passed before I was able to heal and truly know that I was not responsible for what happened.

My stress management strategy during my childhood and early adult years was to go on "automatic pilot." On the outside, the compliant perfectionist and over-achiever parts of me went into overdrive. I tried even harder to be a good, "holy" person, to please everyone, and to do what was expected of me. I chose to attend a college preparatory public high school that was nationally known for its academic excellence. I took the most difficult classes, got good grades, tutored Latin students, participated in after-school activities, baby-sat, and got my first paying job at the age of 13. I put a tremendous amount of pressure on myself to control my feelings, to perform well in everything I did, and to always look good in the process.

In fact, looking good was very much a part of my perfectionist agenda. I remember my parents propping me up in their bed with them when I was very young so I could watch the Miss America Pageant on television. Although I was unaware of it, I locked onto the "Miss America" fantasy as another achievement opportunity and proceeded to win multiple state pageants as a teenager and young adult. I put tremendous pressure on myself to win, despite not having the money, training or other resources that were usually necessary to succeed in this kind of competition. For example, in my first competition, I needed a photo of myself for the program book. Since we didn't have the money to hire a professional photographer, Dad took me to the police station and had his friend, the BCI (Bureau of Criminal Investigation) officer take my picture—you know, the person who takes the mug shots of people who have been arrested! I made it to the Miss America Pageant but I convinced myself that I was doing it for the scholarship money. What I was really doing was performing as a way of getting love and approval. As much as I worked hard to live up to the beauty queen image, I struggled with a deep desire to be seen and accepted as a whole person rather than as a one-dimensional object of admiration or disdain (depending on one's view of people who compete in pageants!).

If there was a way to do anything harder, better, or faster—mostly harder—I found it. In college, I double-majored in pre-med and psychology, worked two 20- to 30-hour a week jobs as a psychiatric research assistant and a residence hall counselor to pay for school, and finished in three and a half years instead of four. After college I continued with psychiatric research work and then moved on to work in social services, higher education, public relations, and high-tech marketing jobs. Most of the jobs were either very demanding and/or included emotionally unhealthy work environments.

On the inside, I beat myself up with endless rounds of negative thinking, especially over-analyzing, worrying and feeling that I had done something wrong. I was overly-serious, gave myself little time for fun, and was painfully self-conscious. My achievements were a way of proving I was a good person, but I never felt "good enough." I numbed myself with quiet anxiety and activity. Beginning at age 13, I also experimented with pot, pills and alcohol as numbing agents.

I was also, as they say, "unlucky in love." When I was in my early 20s I fell in love with someone that I thought was the only person in the world for me. When the relationship did not materialize, I accepted what happened as one of God's punishments, in the belief that I didn't deserve to find happiness in a relationship. After that experience, I often found myself in relationships with men who were troubled, controlling and/or emotionally unavailable. Of course, I was not emotionally available myself. I was not happy with myself so I could not be happy in a relationship. I had no sense of limits and boundaries and found it difficult, if not impossible, to say no. As a result, I was easily taken advantage of by others. I was obsessed with helping others and took pride in people needing me as a way of bolstering my self-worth. I was a classic codependent who played the roles of hero and caretaker.

On a physical level, my free-floating anxiety meant that not only was my mind on alert all the time, but my body was as well. My body was in a constant state of tension. I developed a variety of symptoms and illnesses. My childhood illnesses— headaches, stomachaches and sleeping difficulties—followed me into adulthood where I experienced chronic back pain, psoriasis, TMJ pain, endometriosis, recurring nightmares, night sweats, insomnia and gastrointestinal problems.

In my late 20s, I began to realize that I wasn't finding fulfillment in my work life. Instead of looking inside myself for answers, I decided that, in keeping with my achiever mode, the right thing to do would be to get an MBA. I worked hard to put myself through school and got good grades while I stayed mired in an unstable, extremely codependent relationship. When I graduated, I left that relationship and moved from Rhode Island to Los Angeles to work for a management consulting firm. In keeping with my "harder, better, faster" philosophy, I found myself working 70 to 75 hours a week in the most demanding and unhealthy job environment I had ever experienced. I attained my goal of lasting a year in the job but I paid a huge price. Emotionally, my self-esteem was at an all-time low, my anxiety at an all-time high. Physically, all my childhood and adult illnesses were flaring.

The wake-up call

Then came the wake-up call that I finally paid attention to. (There had been others, but each time I heard one, I rolled over and turned the alarm to snooze.)

After leaving Los Angeles, I returned to Rhode Island, where I was hospitalized several months later with what, I now know, was a stress-related illness. I awoke one morning in excruciating pain and was rushed to the hospital with a gastrointestinal problem. After two days in the hospital and a variety of tests, the doctor could find no physical cause for the symptoms. He eventually asked if there was any stress in my life. I replied, "No, nothing unusual." (Talk about being unconscious!)

He prodded me to tell him more, to which I replied, "I've just given up a very demanding position in Los Angeles as a management consultant to move back to Rhode Island where the market for this work is poor. I'm looking for work and I'm in the middle of planning my wedding. I'm marrying someone that I've only had a long-distance relationship with. He has two teen-age boys, one of whom will live with us. I don't really know the boys because I've been living in California. And, my dearest relative in the world is dying an agonizingly painful death from cancer."

Mmmm. It was beginning to dawn on me that stress might be a problem. The doctor, however, never said another word about stress. He just wrote out a prescription for a stomach medication and suggested staying away from fatty foods. I was confused and dissatisfied. According to my way of thinking, if stress led to my illness, then the medication was only a partial treatment. It only addressed the symptoms I was experiencing, not the underlying problem. What was the treatment supposed to be for the stress I was experiencing?

This was the critical moment when I began to come out of my unconscious haze. My physical illness had made me "teach-able." That is, I was finally willing to question medical authority, to take responsibility for myself, and to participate in my own healing. Beginning with Joan Borysenko's breakthrough book, *Minding the Body, Mending the Mind,* I read everything I could on the mind/body connection. Soon, I realized that my healing needed to take place on more than just a physical level. I needed to heal myself emotionally as well.

My healing journey

Rather than be dependent on a prescription to overcome my physical symptoms that were apparently stress-related, I explored a variety of holistic alternatives—meditation, guided imagery, exercise, low-stress nutrition, and various forms of emotional release work, psychotherapy and energy healing. Within three months, not only did my gastrointestinal problem go away but many of my other stress-related symptoms began to taper off as well. Within six months my physical symptoms were gone. I used to be plagued by headaches three or four times a week, sometimes daily. Now I rarely have a headache. When I do, I use guided visualization techniques and acupressure to relieve the pain. My psoriasis, TMJ pain and endometriosis are under control. A 14-year-long back problem has not reoccurred. The number of colds I have each year has decreased from three to one, sometimes none. At the same time, my 25-year battle with insomnia has significantly improved to the point where it is rarely, if ever, a problem.

Although my emotional healing was more gradual, I did begin to see positive changes in my emotional state within weeks of practicing mind/body/spirit strategies. I learned to look to my emotions as signals that something was out of balance and needed attention. I felt the personal power of seeing options and setting boundaries in difficult situations where previously I would have never considered what was the healthiest alternative for me. I practiced saying "no" when I didn't feel right about something. I also practiced identifying my needs, meeting those needs myself or asking for help. I worked exceptionally hard on dispelling my negative self-talk and feelings of unworthiness by diligently practicing affirmations, self-compassion and self-love. I still remember the amazement I felt when I realized that I wasn't experiencing "free-floating" anxiety on a daily basis. In fact, for a while I was a little confused about not feeling driven by anxiety all the time. Since I was so used to living on an "adrenaline" high, I felt strange without it. I even thought I might be depressed because I was beginning to feel calm inside! Thankfully, I was able to recognize before too long that "calm" was a good thing.

I believe that emotional and spiritual healing is an on-going, life-long process. In this respect, our personal growth is never really done. Once we attain a certain level of safety and peace, however, we can make the journey with much more elegance and ease. What helped me the most in the early stages of my healing work was committing myself to understanding my problems and taking action to overcome them. I read hundreds of self-help books and attended almost as many personal and spiritual growth workshops. More importantly, when the advice from these books and workshops felt right, I incorporated that advice into my personal life and my work life. I allowed myself to reach out to my husband and friends who were committed to their own growth. I found nurturing guidance from a holistic counselor who practiced a form of therapeutic touch called energy work. I also searched for, and developed, a spiritual perspective about the meaning and purpose of life. And finally, I released my beliefs in a punishing, ominous God and embraced a compassionate, loving Divine Power.

Over the years since my healing journey began, I have managed to change my relationship with myself. My first priority is to my own self-love, staying in touch with my Divine connection, and preserving my sense of inner peace. As a result of exploring my feelings about myself and committing myself to accepting, loving and being compassionate with myself, I no longer feel that pervasive sense of "free-floating" anxiety or feelings of unworthiness. On the very few occasions when these emotions do arise, I use them as a signal that something is out of balance in my life. I examine what I'm telling myself and whether I am distorting my thinking in any way. I identify what I'm feeling and then ask myself what need I might have that is not being fulfilled. Then, I make an effort to bring myself back into balance using the strategies that I will share with you in this book.

Because of the relationship I have developed with myself, I am also less likely to view potential stressors as threats and therefore I am able to perceive my environment and the things that happen to me in a more optimistic way. For example, before my emotional healing began I would berate myself mercilessly and feel like a bad person if someone was upset with me for any reason. Now, I accept my humanness and look forward to correcting the problem and learning from the experience. In other words, I look for the opportunity in whatever circumstance I find myself in. I am more accepting of the things I can't change and I feel more powerful to change the things I can. Just as important, I look inside myself and listen to my inner voice in order to determine what is in my highest and best good. In the process of researching and successfully using these mind/body/spirit alternatives for myself, I found my life's work and developed a psychotherapy and seminar practice based on a mind/body/spirit approach to stress management that allows me to "preach what I practice" in a very rewarding way. I am so grateful to have a career that is a natural extension of how I try to live my own life. With my own priorities finally in order I try to teach others what I've learned.

From deep within my inner voice and spiritual knowing, I believe that we all have the opportunity, no matter what challenges or traumas we face, to make the most of our unique talents and capabilities, as well as the circumstances we find ourselves in. Rather than minimize or distort the circumstances of our lives, we need to be open to the role they play in shaping us. Our challenge is to be aware of all the factors that influence us and accept them as opportunities to learn, change and grow. They truly can become the impetus for our becoming stress-resilient, healthy people who can embrace the full breadth of our humanness and all that life has to offer. From a place of healing, I can honestly say that every aspect of my life has provided hidden blessings and contributed in a positive way to who I am now.

One of my greatest satisfactions is being allowed to guide people through the outer aspects of their lives to that place inside where they are connected to their own sense of safety, self-love, inner peace and the Divine. I believe it takes commitment, diligence, a deep sense of gratitude, an openness to all that life has to offer, and of course, the right tools. It is my hope that my approach will provide you with the right tools for your healing journey.

Stress and Change

Change has a monumental effect on the human psyche. Over the last 20 years, we've experienced monumental change. The information and technology explosion, not to mention the breakdown of the nuclear family that has taken place in the last two decades, has accelerated the rate at which we have to integrate change into our lives. This speed of change has had significant psychological repercussions. Books like Alvin Toffler's *Future Shock* and *The Third Wave* describe the devastating effects of this accelerated change on everything from how we learn, travel, work, relate to each other and purchase goods and services, to the way we conduct wars and politics.

Just take the changes that have occurred in travel alone. Beginning in 6,000 B.C., the fastest transportation available was the camel caravan. These camels covered an average of eight miles an hour. By 1938, airplanes could travel at speeds of 400 miles per hour. Twenty years later, rocket planes were traveling 10 times faster, at 4,000 miles per hour, and space capsules nearly five times faster than that, at 18,000 miles per hour. Thanks to tele- and data-communications technology, information now travels around the world—and even to and from outer space—in a matter of seconds. These technological capabilities represent exponential leaps in the progression of change, leaving us to wonder just how much faster the speed of change can go.

The stress of rapid change on the way we live has even led more people to seek therapy. According to a 1987 *New York Times Magazine* article looking at the history of therapy, "the major cause of this past decade's explosive growth in psychotherapy is, most likely, that in these chaotic times, traditional knowledge and customs often provide no good answers to everyday emotional, social and career problems." Even though more people may be seeking help in dealing with stress, current treatment methods are based on ineffective strategies that may not provide the relief that people need.

Drugs and Stress: the Band-aid Approach

There is a drug crisis in this country. It's not only in our streets but in doctors' offices nationwide. Americans are needlessly being medicated by their doctors. Rather than treating the cause, physicians are treating the symptoms of stress with hundreds of millions of prescriptions for antidepressants and tranquilizers worth billions of dollars. The current popular stress management drug "cocktail" might include antidepressant and anti-anxiety medications, such as Prozac, Zoloft or Paxil mixed with Xanax, Klonopin or Ativan. These drugs are not a panacea. They are both psychologically and physically addicting and can produce serious side effects, such as withdrawal, rebound anxiety, insomnia and mental and physical dysfunction (the same symptoms they are supposed to provide relief from). In addition to those just mentioned, the list of possible side effects for these drugs is extensive. The 1996 *Physician's Desk Reference* lists symptoms ranging from headaches, nervousness, sweating, dizziness, nausea, diarrhea, vomiting, rash and itching to chest pains, bleeding, fainting, disorientation, confusion, muscle spasms, tremors, seizures, numbness, hair loss, memory loss, impotence and weight gain.

According to the *The New Harvard Guide to Psychiatry*, there were nearly 100 million prescriptions written in 1988 for benzodiazepines, a class of tranquilizers that includes Xanax, Valium, Klonopin, Ativan, Halcion, Librium and others. And the cost of these prescriptions? Somewhere between $500 and $800 million. The number of prescriptions written each year for antidepressants is growing at an alarming rate. *The Wall Street Journal* reported that as of 1995, Prozac had the unique distinction of being the world's first psychiatric drug to reach $2 billion in annual sales—$2.07 billion to be exact. At the time, Eli Lilly, the company that manufactures Prozac, estimated that this drug had been prescribed for over 21 million people world-wide. The drug accounts for almost one-third of that company's annual sales. Sales for 1997 are expected to reach $2.6 billion. Prozac's chief competitors, Zoloft and Paxil, are expected to earn $1.7 billion and $1.45 billion, respectively. And these are just three drugs! Sales figures for all antidepressant drugs are expected to reach $6 billion by 1998. These numbers would account for over 40 million more people being given prescriptions for antidepressants. What kind of tactics might these companies employ to protect their financial interests?

The economic consequences behind the increasing trend to prescribe this type of medication, not to mention the shocking conflict of interest, are hard to miss, especially when one considers that pharmaceutical companies are major contributors to the American Psychiatric Association and spend multimillions of dollars on sophisticated advertising and public relations campaigns to promote these drugs. Another alarming fact is that pharmaceutical companies are quietly acquiring managed care companies as well as companies that administer the prescription drug component of health insurance plans. This translates into more pressure for drug therapy.

Even more troubling is the fact that many of these drugs are being prescribed by general physicians who are not trained in understanding relevant symptoms or providing critical support services that should accompany drug treatment. According to a 1997 article in *The Wall Street Journal,* many psychiatrists admit that antidepressants are overprescribed for people who don't need them. Often, the only knowledge physicians have about these drugs comes from reading marketing literature provided by the drug companies themselves. Prozac provides a prime example of what's wrong with the system. United Press International reported that more than 80 percent of Prozac prescriptions are written by general physicians who lack psychiatric training. Although Prozac does appear to provide relief for many people, its long-term effects have not yet been determined, and controversy surrounds its use and effectiveness.

Even when tranquilizers, antidepressants and other mood-altering drugs are prescribed by trained psychiatrists, it is often done without considering alternatives to drug therapy. For the most part, psychiatrists then simply monitor the patient during 15-minute office visits every few months. The bottom line is that most doctors don't stop to consider whether there are other effec-tive non-invasive lifestyle and psychotherapeutic strategies that might be employed. Instead, the treatment of choice is to tell the patient to pop some pills.

Now consider how these drugs get approved by the Food and Drug Administration (FDA). The drug companies *themselves* are responsible for conducting drug trials and reporting the re-sults to the FDA. Drugs like Prozac, Xanax and others, although prescribed to millions of people on a long-term basis, are ap-proved by the FDA based on test results with as few as 100 subjects taking the drug for as little as four weeks. Internationally known psychiatrist and author Peter Breggin has long been an outspoken critic of this process. In his books *Toxic Psychiatry* and *Talking Back to Prozac* he describes in detail the serious flaws in these studies and in the drug approval process itself. In *Toxic Psychiatry,* Breggin offers a particularly appalling example from his investigation of the Xanax approval process.

Breggin reports that Xanax, originally purported to be a safe, nonaddicting, antianxiety drug, was tested on 226 subjects for a period of eight weeks. In reading the actual research report he found that the drug company counted only the first four weeks of the study. The drug company discarded the results from sub-sequent weeks, which showed that in a comparison between sub-jects receiving the drug and those receiving a placebo, the drug subjects experienced "severe withdrawal and rebound reactions, including an increase in anxiety and in phobic responses, plus *a 350 percent greater number of panic attacks."* Xanax has since been proven to be highly addicting and has been associated with death when combined with alcohol or other sedatives.

The case for psychiatric medications has clearly not been proven. There is no real proof that chemical imbalances exist in the brain or that they cause mental illness. Current theories about serotonin levels and their effects on mood are based on inference only. There are no medical tests to measure these supposed chemical imbalances.

Dr. Ty Colbert advocates the emotional pain model versus the medical model of mental illness. He believes, as I and a growing number of other professionals do, that mental illness is not biologically based, but is a reflection of a person's emotional woundedness. In his book, *Broken Brains or Wounded Hearts*, Dr. Colbert extensively examines the evidence supporting the medical model of mental illness and concludes:

> . . . the truth is that researchers have never discovered a single defective gene or accurately identified any chemical imbalance that has caused an emotional disorder; nor have they ever proven that brain abnormalities are responsible for *even one* emotional disorder. In fact, the National Institute of Mental Health openly admits that the causes of schizophrenia, depression, mania, anxiety, and hyperactivity are unknown.

The purpose of psychiatric drugs is to control symptoms. They do not address the cause of the symptoms.

Prescription drugs as a treatment for stress and anxiety are only a "Band-Aid" approach. Although drugs may provide short-term relief, they preempt an individual's motivation to understand and overcome the underlying problem. In some cases, people are being given prescriptions for medication when they are going through normal stresses of life—as if it were abnormal to feel grief when we lose a loved one or a job or to feel anxious when we make life changes like getting a divorce or raising children. For some people, taking a pill translates into a personal belief that there is something elementally wrong with them or that they are incapable of solving their own problems. It encourages people to numb out their bad feelings just as they would with over-eating, smoking, alcohol and street drugs. At its worst, taking pills teaches people that they are helpless to cope with their feelings without the help of mood-altering drugs.

Not everyone wants to or needs to take a pill to manage stress, nor is it in their best interest to do so. The current "instant fix" being prescribed by physicians is leaving people feeling powerless over their own bodies and hopeless about their ability to control their lives. There *is* a better way. Not only is there a better way, but it could save billions of dollars in unwarranted medication and treatment costs as well as help people regain control over their lives.

Warning: Withdrawing suddenly from psychiatric medications can cause serious emotional and physical reactions and should only be undertaken with medical supervision.

Mind/Body Programs: A Better Way

Medical and psychological experts are giving more credence to the fact that traditional approaches that attend only to the body or the mind fall short in alleviating stress-related problems on a long-term basis. Clearly the mind and body are intimately related. Research has demonstrated that every thought we think produces a chemical reaction in the brain that is transmitted to every cell in the body. This amazing exchange of information happens within seconds. In order to be effective in treating the stress response, clinicians need to be trained in both psychology and medicine. The more successful therapeutic approaches to stress management incorporate the interplay between mind and body into stress management techniques that work.

Herbert Benson's Mind/Body Clinic at New England Deaconness Hospital in Boston and Jon Kabat-Zinn's Stress Reduction Program at the University of Massachusetts Medical Center in Worcester, Massachusetts are two successful examples of an integrated mind/body approach. Patients enter these eight- to ten-week programs with a wide variety of problems including asthma, gastrointestinal disturbances, premenstrual syndrome, chronic pain, anxiety, depression, insomnia, cardiac disease, cancer, AIDS and many other illnesses. As program participants they are given instruction in relaxation training, exercise, nutrition and stress management. Outcome studies for both of these programs prove that this kind of approach is more effective than traditional medical protocols alone.

Patients with chronic pain report significant reductions in pain and related symptoms such as anxiety and depression.

Those with hypertension experience significant decreases in blood pressure and need fewer medications. Migraine and headache sufferers have fewer and less severe headaches. One study showed that insomnia was cured in 75 percent of participants while the remaining 25 percent experienced improved sleep. Another study showed that women suffering from premenstrual syndrome experienced a 57 percent decrease in severity of symptoms. After completing the program, patients with anxiety or depression are less anxious, depressed, angry and hostile. On the job, people also experience reduced symptoms of depression, anxiety and hostility as well as fewer medical symptoms and sick days, improved performance and lower blood pressure. Patients with AIDS and cancer experience decreased symptoms and better control of the nausea and vomiting associated with chemotherapy.

My own survey of private practice clients echoed these results. Clients were selected at random to receive the survey by mail. No incentives were offered, and participation was completely anonymous. Seventy-four clients who had practiced the strategies outlined in this book for a period of two months to four years responded to the survey. Of those who responded:

o 93 percent were aware of improved emotional and physical health.
o 78 percent achieved a level of inner peace, while an additional 21 percent said they were more aware of their need for inner peace and the strategies that would help them achieve it.
o 93 percent said they managed stress more effectively than prior to adopting the *Strategies for Health and Inner Peace* approach.

With very few exceptions, my clients are also able to significantly reduce or eliminate their reliance on medications for symptom relief.

What Is Stress and How Can We Manage It?

Most people think they know what stress is. Stress is the boss, the weather, finances, the car breaking down, pain, illness, etc. But these things do not create stress in and of themselves. We know this because what may be stressful for you today may not be stressful for you tomorrow, and because, what may be stressful for you is not necessarily stressful for someone else. Some people experience stress in the presence of snakes, others don't. Some people experience stress when their bills aren't paid, others don't. Likewise, what causes an individual stress today, may not do so tomorrow. For example, waking up to newly fallen snow on a work day may be stressful because you tell yourself you have to shovel your car out to get to an important business meeting. On the other hand, waking up to a newly fallen snow on a day that you're going skiing may be exhilarating because you tell yourself that the skiing conditions will be great. Stress is an individual experience because of what we tell ourselves about the situation we find ourselves in. And, what we tell ourselves about the situation in that moment is influenced by a variety of things including psychological, social, environmental and physical factors.

The definition of stress continues to evolve. Over the last 50 years, researchers have learned more about stress, its effects, and how to address these effects. While certain aspects of the definition continue to be debated, most experts now agree that there is a distinction between stress and stressors. I define these two concepts in the following way:

o Stressors are situations, conditions, people, or things that have the *potential* to trigger the stress response in us.
o Stress occurs when we tell ourselves something negative about ourselves and our ability to cope with a particular stressor. In psychological terms, we experience stress when we tell ourselves that a particular stressor is a threat to us in some way.

This distinction will help you understand the stress management program outlined in this book. It is based on the understanding that we cannot necessarily control what happens to us (that is, the stressors we encounter), but we *can* control how we *perceive* what happens to us. Subsequently, we can then control how we react to what happens to us. To manage stress, we must begin with our perceptions about ourselves and our ability to cope with what happens to us. These perceptions determine the degree of stress we will experience or whether we will experience stress at all. *What we tell ourselves about ourselves* then, is the key to understanding and managing stress.

The Mind/Body Connection

In order to comprehend the importance of managing stress it's also important to know that the mind has a very direct impact on the body. When we tell ourselves that we are being threatened in some way, the mind tells the body, through a series of electrochemical reactions, to prepare to cope with the threat. The body's reaction to a perceived threat is called the *fight/flight response* or the *stress response*. During the stress response, powerful hormones in the form of adrenaline, cortisol and steroids, are released into the bloodstream. These hormones allow the body to achieve a heightened state of alertness and readiness to defend itself. If triggered long enough or often enough, the body begins to exhaust itself, causing an increased risk of illness. The existence of the stress response gives us a clear indication that the mind and body are intimately connected. We'll learn more about the connection between illness and the stress response in the chapters ahead.

Types of Stressors

The experience of stress can be brief, such as when we slam on the brakes to avoid something in the road. It can be periodic, such as when we gear up for intermittent deadlines at work. It can also be chronic, such as when we are caring for a sick person or living in an abusive relationship. The severity and intensity of stressors can also vary. For example, being raped or witnessing a traumatic event may be considered an acute stressor because it occurs only once, but the recurring memories of the event may be considered chronic stressors. Research has proven that even minor acute stressors, such as taking an exam, can affect the immune system negatively and produce a variety of symptoms. So even small amounts of stress can have an adverse effect on health.

Physical conditions may also become stressors based on what we tell ourselves about them and our ability to cope with them. For example, suppose you told yourself that your racing heart was dangerous. This threatening thought could trigger the stress response. Not only would you experience stress, but the stress response would likely exacerbate your racing heart symptom.

While we have been focusing on a class of stressors created by our perceptions, there are certain substances and external conditions that can be considered stressors based on the body's reaction to them. Physical conditions that disrupt the body's homeostasis such as exposure to extreme temperatures and lack of oxygen, as well as ingesting caffeine, nicotine, alcohol, cocaine, diet pills and other drugs can trigger the stress response. Negative or distorted thinking about the effects of these substances and physical conditions can then exacerbate the stress response.

Thoughts and Beliefs

Understanding that stress, for the most part, begins with our thoughts and beliefs is the first step in figuring out ways to manage it effectively. To begin, we must first identify our own unique stressors. Then we must examine what thoughts and beliefs cause these stressors to be threatening to us. When we tell ourselves something negative about our ability to deal with a potential stressor, we are telling ourselves that we cannot cope with or control the situation. One of the keys to effective stress management is understanding that we cannot control every potential stressor that occurs in our lives, regardless of its source. What we *can* control is our reaction to that stressor, based on what we tell ourselves about ourselves and our ability to cope with the situation we find ourselves in.

In examining the thoughts and beliefs that underlie our unique stressors, it is important to distinguish between thoughts based on the past and thoughts based on our present experiences. In many instances, the thoughts and beliefs that create stress in the present are a result of past programming. Negative childhood experiences, from being shamed or criticized by a caretaker or ridiculed by peers to more traumatic experiences such as living with an emotionally and/or physically abusive caretaker, helped shape our view of ourselves today. Often, these negative or traumatic experiences create thought and belief patterns that program us for low self-worth and low self-esteem as adults. If we allow these experiences to go unexamined and unresolved they can become unconscious and automatic. Under these circumstances, our thoughts and perceptions become distorted and we may react to potential stressors based on these unconscious, automatic beliefs rather than on our strengths as adults in the present moment.

When we evaluate our programming and become more accepting, loving and compassionate with ourselves, we change. We tend to view potential stressors as opportunities rather than as threats. Having a positive relationship with ourselves means that we can look inward for our sense of self-worth and self-esteem. We no longer have to rely on programming from others to determine how we think and feel about ourselves. In looking inward, we can begin to develop that sense of safety that says, "I can't control everything that happens to me but I can control how I react to it." By thinking and feeling positively about ourselves in the present moment, by being in touch with that sense of inner safety, our fear and anxiety decrease and we can begin to feel a sense of inner peace.

Strategies for Health and Inner Peace

The term "holistic" often refers to the relationship and integration of mind, body and spirit. After a 300-year separation of psychology and medical science, the mind/body/spirit connection is finally being addressed once again in medicine. Behavioral medicine grew out of the work of a relatively new field of science called psychoneuroimmunology (PNI), which combines the disciplines of neuroscience, psychology and immunology. Behavioral medicine recognizes that mental and emotional factors can have a significant effect on our physical health and on our capacity to recover from illness and injury.

Emerging evidence from PNI research supports a holistic approach to stress that recognizes the mind/body/spirit connection in both an individual and social context. In their book, *Controlling Stress and Tension*, leading researchers Daniel Girdano, George Everly and Dorothy Dusek offer their definition of holistic stress management as "a concept of controlling stress and tension encompassing the complete lifestyle of the individual," one which ". . . incorporates intervention at the physical, psychological and social levels simultaneously." Their solution supports a preventive approach which recognizes that perceptions, behavior, emotions, personality, environment, social interactions and spirituality all play a role in the body's response to stress.

Holistic approaches to stress management continue to gain acceptance and validity among those practicing traditional medicine as well as those seeking treatment. This book was written to substantiate and foster that interest.

I've used the latest information and research to develop a stress management model that centers on an individual's ability and power to participate in his or her own healing. My approach is a holistic one that acknowledges the connection between the mind, the body and the human spirit. It is founded on a rationale that combines psychological and medical evidence to support this unique and complex connection.

Please note that this work is not meant to be a replacement for traditional medicine or psychotherapy. It is meant to be an important complement to these and other methods of emotional and physical healing.

The core of my approach is learning to become aware of and to understand one's own unique mind/body stress signals. These include physical, emotional, cognitive and spiritual factors. My approach emphasizes self-awareness, self-acceptance and self-compassion as motivation for positive behavior change. I teach people to listen to their bodies and inner voices, to develop self-love and inner validation, to experience inner peace and to learn how to heal themselves. I encourage those who are receptive to develop a sense of connectedness with others and a Divine Power, whatever they envision that to be. I "practice what I preach" and I never ask anyone to do anything I haven't done myself.

My clients are people experiencing a wide variety of emotional challenges from life changes, relationship and self-esteem issues to abuse and trauma issues. I also work with people who are experiencing physical ailments such as migraines, chronic pain, TMJ, high blood pressure, anxiety attacks, irritable bowel syndrome, back pain, allergies, chronic fatigue, fibromyalgia, heart disease, cancer and other stress-related illnesses.

I never cease to be amazed by my clients' abilities to change and to heal themselves. Those who believe in and commit to their own personal power and the mind/body/spirit strategies I teach them often begin to experience relief from emotional and physical symptoms in a relatively short time. In cases of chronic conditions or illnesses, clients often feel an enhanced ability to cope with and manage their symptoms.

As I mentioned earlier, with very few exceptions, my clients are also able to significantly reduce or eliminate their reliance on medications for symptom relief as they become more aware of, and learn to satisfy, their own emotional, physical and spiritual needs. As a result of committing to this work, many of my clients have experienced a disappearance of free-floating anxiety and an increased sense of inner peace just as I have by practicing the techniques described in this book.

Where You Can Begin

To manage your stress, improve your health, and ultimately gain a sense of inner peace, you must be willing to make a commitment to yourself to manage your stress. You must also be willing to risk thinking and behaving in healthier, more effective ways. Remember, as Wayne Dyer has said, *"You don't have to be sick to get better."*

We need stress management techniques the most, when we are least able to use them. The time to learn to manage stress is now. Learning preventive strategies and incorporating them into our lifestyle before stress becomes a problem will ensure that when stress does arise, we will have healthy coping mechanisms already in place and easily available to us.

This book emphasizes a balanced lifestyle approach, which takes into account physical, mental, emotional and spiritual health issues. When you finish reading and begin to practice the strategies in the book you will:

o Understand the mind/body/spirit stress relationship
o Recognize your unique stressors and how you react to them

○ Learn techniques that mediate the experience of stress and also reduce and reverse its negative effects

○ Open yourself to experiencing better health and more inner peace

The purpose of this book is to provide a framework for stress management that includes the latest information and techniques available. Moreover, it provides the means for you to incorporate this information and these techniques into a more balanced lifestyle. The strength of the work lies in its holistic perspective and, therefore, is not meant to be applied as a collection of disconnected techniques. As a whole, it will provide you with the opportunity to understand stress, not as an isolated set of symptoms, but with a more global scope, involving you as a whole person in relation to yourself, others and your environment.

What Research Tells Us
About Stress

The Early Years

Stress has been a hot topic among researchers for more than 30 years. Despite this attention, there is still much debate over exactly how to define stress. Early stress researchers identified three distinct categories of stress: physiological, psychological and social. But few, if any, studies attempted to combine these categories into one experimental design. Some recent researchers have included philosophical and spiritual factors as contributors to stress. Two important ideas emerged from early stress research that are significant to today's holistic approaches to stress management:

○ Stress and illness are linked.
○ Understanding stress requires understanding a variety of complex interactions, including mental, emotional, physical and spiritual factors.

Physiological psychologist Hans Selye first brought the term "stress" into the domain of psychology in the 1950s. He built on the earlier work of physiologists Claude Bernard in the 1850s and Walter Cannon in the 1920s. Bernard identified the importance of an organism's ability to maintain a constant internal environment even as its external environment changed. Cannon then coined the term "homeostasis," which refers to the ability of an organism to maintain a state of equilibrium or balance. Through his own laboratory work, Selye defined stress as "the nonspecific response of the body to any demand upon it."

Selye identified two major occurrences that happened when a demand was placed on an animal or human. First, he noted a specific response to the demand. Examples would be shivering in response to cold or perspiring in response to heat. He also believed that no matter what the demand or trauma, the body would always have an accompanying stereotypical hormonal response. He termed this a nonspecific response. In other words, Selye believed that any stressor could trigger the stress response and that the level and degree of the stress response was always the same.

Another critical aspect of Selye's work was his identification of a connection between stress and disease. Based on his studies of what happens to animals when they are injured or placed under extreme conditions, Selye developed the theory of the General Adaptation Syndrome (GAS). GAS describes a stress response that occurs when a demand or trauma is not withdrawn. According to this theory, if the stress response continues unabated, it will ultimately lead to diseases that can progress to exhaustion and even death.

Although Selye's definition of stress went unchallenged for many years, by the 1960s researchers developed evidence that questioned Selye's nonspecific stress response. The controversy focused on the possibility that the stress response is a psychophysiological phenomenon dependent on several factors, including characteristics specific to a given stressor as well as the individual experiencing the stressor. By 1965, research evidence indicated that individuals subjected to the same type of stressor will not necessarily respond in the same way. Moreover, an individual may not necessarily respond in the same way to the same stressor at any given time. These findings led the way toward consideration of a model of stress that looked at individual differences and how these differences might be involved in the stress response.

Researchers have since developed evidence suggesting that the stress response is triggered by psychological responses to a demand or trauma, that the stress response can be attenuated by psychological factors, and that hormonal responses are affected by how a person relates to his environment. These findings support Richard Lazarus' transactional model that defined stress as occurring in the face of "demands that tax or exceed the resources of the system." In human terms, Lazarus decided that psychological stress depended on what the individual demands of himself or herself.

Other studies have focused on the social determinants of stress. These have ranged from studies of people in natural disasters, on the battlefield and in isolation, to those in specific job situations such as astronauts and air traffic controllers. The 1967 Holmes and Rahe study published in *Psychosomatic Research*, is probably the most widely known in terms of understanding stress in a social context. In their research, they found that people are more likely to develop illnesses following periods of stressful life changes such as the death of a spouse, divorce or retirement. However, more research is still needed in order to determine exactly how physiological, psychological and social factors may be linked to the stress response.

Lazarus recognized the need for this kind of research over 30 years ago. As a result, he developed an interdisciplinary view of the field of stress that is still relevant today:

> It seems wise to use "stress" as a generic term for the whole area of problems that includes the stimuli producing stress reactions, the reactions themselves, and the various intervening processes. Thus we can speak of the field of stress and mean the physiological, sociological, and psychological phenomena and their respective concepts.

Current Theories of Stress

A review of the literature to date shows that the transactional approach to stress is still widely supported and appears to be the framework for current stress theory and research. Building on this model, most researchers also appear to agree on a critical aspect of the conditions under which stress occurs. There is a consensus that stress occurs when an individual makes a cognitive appraisal of a situation or condition and decides that a demand/capability imbalance exists. Simply put, an individual experiences stress when he is presented with a potential stressor (person, place, event, etc.) and tells himself that he is unable to cope effectively with that stressor.

With this understanding, researchers again moved away from Selye's view of the stress response as nonspecific and began to address the question of why some people are more susceptible to stress than others. Once researchers studied the stress response as a cognitive appraisal process (i.e., as a thought process), they identified a variety of factors that play a role in an individual's assessment of potential stressors. For the most part, these include and are described as attitudes toward the source of stress, prior experience with the stressor, risk/threat assessment, assessment of personal and environmental resources, emotional needs and values, stress vulnerability, feedback, adaptation and magnitude/ intensity of the demand.

Cognitive theorists such as Albert Ellis amended the cognitive appraisal theory of stress with an important consideration. Ellis agreed that we experience stress because of what we tell ourselves about ourselves and our environment but added that *many of these thoughts are based on irrational beliefs.*

Although the transactional model resulted in many hypothetical concepts that describe an array of complex psychophysiological interactions, there remains a lack of evidence from well-designed experiments in psychology and psychophysiology that control for these mind/body parameters.

Physiological Research

While psychology and psychobiology offer limited integrated research on stress, psychoneuroimmunology (PNI) research is focused on the psychophysiological determinants of stress and how stress is linked to disease and illness.

PNI research began with the work of Robert Ader. Ader is credited with accidentally discovering that the immune system could be influenced by what an individual believed, that is, by what went on in the brain. In 1974, the conventional view held that the immune system was a self-regulating system and therefore outside the realm of conscious control. This view was seriously challenged when Ader was conducting a classical conditioning experiment and found that the rats in his study had learned to suppress their own immune systems and were dying as a result.

Another critical research development, which provided additional evidence of the mind-body connection, was the discovery of neurotransmitters, in particular, endorphins. Neurotransmitters are the chemical messengers that the brain uses to communicate with the body. In 1986, Candace Pert published evidence suggesting that neurotransmitters, which also play a key role in regulating the internal physiology of the body, had specific receptor sites throughout the body. According to Pert, neurotransmitters in the brain transmit messages between cells that trigger the release of neurohormones, which then travel through the bloodstream to receptor sites in specific organs.

Research also shows that certain neurotransmitters, such as endorphins, play a role in mediating the stress response. Endorphins are a distinct category of neurotransmitters that affect feeling states, such as relief of pain, relief of fatigue and a feeling of energy. They are found in high concentration in the pituitary, the gland responsible for secreting the hormones that regulate bodily functions. This information not only supported the concept of a mind/body connection, it also identified an actual mechanism for psychophysiological communication—the way the mind talks to the body.

PNI research findings to date, while not completely conclusive, suggest that:

o The mind and body are intimately connected.
o The mind and body communicate with one another via a complex mechanism of electrical and chemical messages.
o The brain regulates the body via this electrochemical mechanism.
o The brain, the immune system and the neuroendocrine system are also interconnected via this mechanism.
o It is possible to gain voluntary control over the immune system.
o The brain, via the hypothalamus and its production of neurohormones, plays a role in triggering and mediating the stress response.

Stress Can Make You Sick

The underlying theory for much of today's PNI work centers on the following:

○ Stress can suppress the immune system.
○ Stress can suppress the immune system enough to increase an individual's risk of developing physical illness.
○ Mind/body/spirit approaches to stress management are effective not only in boosting resistance to illness but in treating illness as well.

PNI researchers are focusing on identifying how the physiological changes that occur under stress affect and are directly linked to disease and illness. In addition, they are also looking at the correlations between certain psychological factors and certain illnesses. Many studies have examined what factors might predict who is susceptible to illnesses ranging from the common cold and mononucleosis to heart disease and cancer.

The Common Cold

In 1991, the *New England Journal of Medicine* reported a connection between stress and the common cold. In the study, subjects were exposed to a cold virus via a nasal spray. Subjects who were under stress prior to the study (as determined by a questionnaire) were more than twice as likely to catch a cold as those who were not under stress. The implication here is that exposure to a cold virus is not sufficient in and of itself to cause illness. Rather stress is a determining factor in our susceptibility to illness.

Mononucleosis

In 1979, researchers Kasel, Evans and Niederman of West Point reported the results of a study they conducted on the development of infectious mononucleosis in the journal *Psychosomatic Medicine*. This study also shows a link between stress and illness. Over a four-year period, cadets were periodically screened for the presence of Epstein-Barr antibodies, which are the body's response to infection with the E-B virus. Results showed that approximately one-fifth of the cadets screened were infected with Epstein-Barr antibodies, but only 25 percent of those infected actually became ill with mono. The researchers, who collected demographic and psychological information about the cadets, found that stress was a determining factor in whether they became ill or not. The cadets who developed mono had "high stress" profiles.

Herpes

In a 1993 review of studies that relate herpes virus activity and stress, Janice Kiecolt-Glaser and Ronald Glaser concluded that "these studies provide consistent and convincing evidence that stress can affect the body's control over herpes virus infections." The studies identified the level of herpes virus antibodies in the blood as a measure of immune system function, with high levels of antibodies indicating low immune system function.

One study showed that medical students had higher levels of herpes virus antibodies when they were taking exams as opposed to when they were on summer vacation. In another, people who were divorced or separated showed a higher level of antibodies than did a control group of married people. In two separate studies, it was found that psychiatric inpatients and people who were caregivers for family members with Alzheimer's disease had more herpes virus antibodies than control groups. In still another study, it was reported that depression was a likely precursor in the frequency of recurrence of genital herpes.

Heart Disease

Heart disease is the leading cause of death in the United States. As such, it has been the focus of a tremendous amount of research. Findings to date provide convincing evidence that stress and emotions, such as hostility and anger, play a significant role in the development of heart disease. In the late 1960s, cardiologist Meyer Friedman identified a link between a behavior pattern he termed Type A and the development of heart disease. Type A is generally characterized in terms of hurriedness, competitiveness and hostility—a high-stress personality profile. Research subjects labeled Type A were found twice as likely to develop heart disease as those who were not labeled Type A. Further studies have failed to replicate the Type A findings consistently, leading researchers to focus on specific aspects of Type A behavior.

Many well-known studies have shown a link specifically between hostility and heart disease. In the 1950s researcher Robert Shekelle found that high hostility was a significant predictor of increased risk of heart attack or other symptoms of heart disease for male employees at Western Electric. The Western Electric study findings were also confirmed in a 25-year study of doctors conducted by John Barefoot. Barefoot found that doctors with high hostility scores, as indicated on a psychological test, were four to five times more likely to develop heart disease than those with low scores. In yet another study, researcher Redford Williams found that subjects with high hostility scores also had the most coronary blockage. In fact, over 70 percent of subjects with high scores had severe blockages.

People under stress and those who score as hostile have similar physiological symptoms that put them at risk for heart disease. People in both categories have been shown to have greater increases in blood pressure and stress hormone levels, such as adrenaline and cortisol, than people who are not stressed and do not score as hostile. Another of cardiologist Friedman's studies measured the blood-clotting and cholesterol levels of accountants during and after tax season. As expected, both measures increased and reached their highest levels just prior to April 15. The levels decreased and returned to normal following the tax deadline. Stress hormones caused the blood to clot and trigger rises in blood pressure and blood cholesterol levels. Both high blood cholesterol and high blood pressure are critical risk factors in the development of heart disease.

Immune System Functions

In their article *Mind and Immunity* noted psychologist Janice Kiecold-Glaser and immunologist Ronald Glaser offer a review of a number of studies they and others have conducted examining the link between stress and the immune system. Evidence indicates that even short-term stress, such as taking an exam, can affect immune system function. In an annual study of medical students, researchers found that students exhibited a significant decline in the growth and activity of natural killer (NK) cells during exam time. In a separate study conducted with medical students at exam time, students showed significant increases in the stress hormones adrenaline and noradrenalin.

Researchers have also looked at the effects of prolonged and intense stress on immune system function. Astronauts, widows, and people who have been sleep-deprived all showed decreased immune system function. One study showed widowers' immune system function dropped significantly within two months of the death of their spouses and, in some, remained low for as long as ten months afterward. Other studies showed that widowers were more likely to die within six months of their spouse's death. Long-term caregivers of Alzheimer's patients also showed a decrease in immune function. These caregivers continued to show this decrease even after the patient died. Caregivers also developed more illnesses than those in a control group.

Other emotional and social conditions also appear to have a negative impact on immune system functioning. In a review of data from several well-controlled studies, sociologist James House and his colleagues concluded that stressful social relationships competed with smoking, high blood pressure, high blood cholesterol, obesity and physical inactivity as a risk factor for illness and early death. In separate studies using a variety of subjects, including adolescents, medical students and psychiatric patients, Kiecolt-Glaser and her colleagues showed a connection between loneliness and decreased activity of NK immune cells. In 1984, Stephen Locke and his colleagues reported that anxiety and depression were also associated with decreased activity of NK cells. Other studies have linked decreased immune function with divorce, separation and unhappiness in marriage, bereavement, pessimism and expressed need for power and control.

What Makes Us Stress-Resilient?

Although many studies show a link between stress and illness, the connection is not a simple one. From the 1950s to the 1970s, researchers looked at possible links between behavior patterns and certain illnesses such as Type-A personality and heart disease. The evidence to support such links has not been conclusive. This may be due, in part, to the fact that each individual is made up of a complex set of traits and experiences that makes it hard to generalize from one individual to the next. We also know that people's behavior cannot readily be predicted. As indicated before, different people react differently to the same stressors, and an individual may not always react the same way to the same stressor. To complicate matters even further, some people exposed to stress get ill and others do not. This has led researchers to ask: What protects some people from the ill effects of stress and not others? Evidence to date indicates that certain cognitive, emotional, social and spiritual factors contribute to illness, recovery and health. Thus, researchers are now investigating how attitudes, beliefs and emotions may play a critical role in determining who stays healthy and who gets sick.

In previous chapters we learned that the immune system responds to messages from the brain. While many studies have focused on identifying negative factors that inhibit the immune system and lead to illness, many other studies now offer evidence that certain positive factors keep us healthy and help us recover when we do get sick. The real power behind stress resiliency lies in our beliefs and abilities to cope with stress. Let's look more closely at those factors that defend us against the ill effects of stress and enhance immune functioning.

Stress Hardiness

Certain attitudes and coping strategies play a key role in determining how people experience stress and whether people under stress develop illnesses. In 1979 Suzanne Kobasa coined the term "stress hardy" as a result of a study she conducted with middle- to upper-level executives. In the study, executives who became ill had a strong sense of alienation and powerlessness and felt threatened by change. Conversely, those executives who remained healthy in the face of similar stressors exhibited the "stress hardy" characteristics of commitment, challenge and control. In this study, commitment referred to a sense of involvement and meaning in what was happening in an individual's life; challenge referred to the ability to see life changes and stressors as opportunities; and control referred to a belief that one had influence over his/her life.

In a later study, Kobasa found that the combination of certain qualities was an even stronger predictor of who got sick and who did not. Hardy executives who exercised and had strong social support had less than an 8 percent chance of getting sick, as opposed to a 93 percent chance for those who did not have these same attributes. These findings provide an important reminder that the mind/body connection, particularly the link between stress and illness, is hardly a simple one.

Control

One aspect of stress hardiness has received a great deal of attention—the issue of control versus helplessness. In several studies with animals, the experimental design consisted of three groups. The first group received shocks they could learn to escape from, signifying control. The second group received inescapable shocks, signifying no control. The third group received no shock. Later, all three groups were tested for their ability to learn to avoid shock.

In 1975 Martin Seligman identified the "learned help-lessness" theory as a result of his research findings that dogs subjected to inescapable shock failed to learn to escape it in subsequent trials where escape was possible. Another researcher studied rats injected with cancerous tumor cells and found that only 27 percent of the rats exposed to inescapable shock rejected their tumors as compared to 70 percent of those who could escape the shock. Surprisingly, the latter group fared even better than the control group (who experienced no shocks at all), where only 50 percent rejected their tumors. The inferences here are that the ability to control or manage stress may somehow boost the immune system and that learned helplessness, as a psychological state, may be connected to the development of cancer.

In 1977 psychologists Ellen Langer and Judith Rodin reported their findings regarding the issue of learned helplessness in humans. Langer and Rodin conducted a landmark study with nursing home residents as subjects. One group of residents was given a certain amount of control over their lives, such as what they could eat and what they could do for recreation. A second group of residents was not given these choices. After 18 months, residents who were given control were measured as happier and more active than the residents who were not given control. Additionally, only 15 percent of residents in the group with "control" had died as compared to 30 percent of the residents in the "no control" group.

In his book, *Healthy Work: Stress, Productivity and the Reconstruction of Working Life,* Robert Karasek establishes a link between control and heart disease as it relates to a person's job. He describes evidence indicating that those people who experienced little or no control over the demand of their jobs were significantly more likely to develop heart disease than those who experienced a greater sense of control over the demands of their work. And the jobs that ranked the highest for incidence of heart disease? Bus drivers, air traffic controllers and secretaries.

Self-Efficacy

Self-efficacy refers to a person's belief in his/her ability to achieve a specific goal or master a challenge. One's perceived ability to control a situation is also an important aspect of self-efficacy. In order to test the connection between stress, immune function and self-efficacy, subjects with a snake phobia were taught to cope with their fear of snakes. Coping skills included mastering a series of steps involved in overcoming their phobia. Evidence showed that as subjects increased their levels of self-efficacy, their heart rate and cortisol (a stress hormone) levels decreased, while their immune function increased. Thus, as people felt more positive about their ability to deal with their fear, they experienced less stress and better immune function.

Optimism

The subject of optimism and health has also been the focus of a variety of studies. According to Seligman and others, optimists do not blame themselves for bad events that happen to them. They believe that these bad events will be temporary and they view these events as specific to a particular area of their lives. In other words, they do not globalize problems in one area of their lives as a means of believing that everything in their lives is going wrong.

The 35-year Harvard Study of Adult Development Project found that men who scored high on optimism were healthier later in life than those who scored low on optimism. Other studies on optimism involved the effect of optimism on the immune system. In another Seligman study, researchers rated a group of men and women on their level of optimism, then drew blood samples. As expected, those who scored as optimists had better immune activity than those who scored as pessimists. In other studies of heart disease and cancer patients, those who scored high on optimism, despite the severity of illness, were more likely to be long-term survivors.

Hope

Other researchers have looked at how hopefulness relates to the development and progression of illness. In this context, hope refers to an individual's determination to meet goals and his ability to create plans to achieve those goals. One study looked at hopefulness versus hopelessness as a factor in predicting cervical cancer. The subjects were women who had undergone cervical biopsies to evaluate abnormal pap smears. Based on the patients' hopelessness scores, researchers successfully predicted 68 percent of those who tested positive for cancer and 77 percent of those who tested negative. A Virginia Commonwealth University study examined how hope affected the quality of life of patients paralyzed from spinal cord injuries. The results indicated that those who scored high on a measure of hope did better emotionally and physically than did those who scored low, even when the level of injury was the same.

Expressing Emotions

The role of emotions in the development and progression of cancer have also been the focus of many studies. In an 18-year study of 1,330 Johns Hopkins University medical students, Dr. Caroline Thomas examined whether certain illnesses could be predicted by physical exams and psychological tests. Her findings showed that those who developed cancer scored lowest on tests for depression, anxiety and anger. Some interpret Thomas's findings in combination with other research as evidence that cancer patients may indeed experience these emotions, but tend to suppress them. Psychologists Lydia Temoshok and Andrew Knier measured the responses of cancer patients and heart disease patients when receiving a mild electric shock. Although the cancer patients had stronger physical reactions than the heart disease patients, they appeared to minimize reports of their emotional upset to researchers after the test. Temoshok later postulated that cancer patients are likely to be uncomplaining, cooperative and resistant to expressing emotions and termed these traits Type-C personality. In some studies cancer patients were able to express anger and hostility on behalf of someone else but appeared unable to express anger or hostility on behalf of themselves. This is in contrast to the Type-A personality associated with heart disease, in that heart disease patients tend to overexpress their anger and hostility.

In a study of breast cancer patients, researchers found that long-term survivors expressed higher levels of anxiety, hostility, guilt, depression and alienation than short-term survivors. The long-term survivors also expressed more negative attitudes toward their illness. It is important to note here that from a psychological perspective, it would be considered healthy for people with cancer to have and appropriately express feelings of anxiety, anger, hostility or depression toward their illness.

In a separate study researchers found that women with breast cancer had four different reactions to the disease. Some women thoroughly denied the seriousness of their illness while others adopted the attitude that they would learn everything they could in order to fight and conquer the disease. Other women were either indifferent to the diagnosis or gave up entirely. Differences in survival rates for these various groups of women were significant. Seventy-five percent of the women who reacted with denial or a fighting spirit were alive five years later as compared to only 35 percent of the women who reacted indifferently or gave up completely. These findings indicate that those who are able to express their emotions, even emotions that may be considered negative, not only live longer, but as Thomas' study implies, may be more resistant to developing cancer in the first place. Still, research in this area is not complete, and we remain in the exploratory stages of understanding the relationship between expressing emotions and the development of illness.

Sharing one's feelings can also have a positive affect on the immune system. In one of the first studies to examine shared feelings, college students who were asked to write about traumatic events experienced higher immune system function and a greater drop in visits to the health center, as compared to students who wrote about trivial events. Those students who wrote about events they had never revealed before to anyone showed the most improvement.

Social Support

Just as the lack of social support has been connected with lowered immune system functioning and illness, a high degree of social support has been specifically linked to longer survival times, recovery and health. In 1989, Dr. David Spiegel conducted a 10-year study of the effects of group support on women with advanced breast cancer. He found that those women who participated in group support meetings lived an average of 18 months longer than those who did not participate in group support. At the time of the study, a woman with advanced breast cancer had a life expectancy of only 18 months, so these findings indicated that group support actually doubled the survival time for the disease. According to Dr. Spiegel, the effectiveness of group support far exceeded that of any medication or medical treatment available at the time.

Spirituality

Research in the area of spirituality and health is just beginning. By its very nature, it is difficult to study and to measure scientifically. Several researchers, however, have attempted to address these issues. In one study of cancer patients, spiritual beliefs were associated with better pain control and sense of well-being, but not with longer survival. Another study showed that religious beliefs were important to 90 percent of the subjects during their illness. David McClelland attempted to measure spiritual qualities such as love, altruism and caring. He showed subjects films either about Mother Teresa's work with the poor or Attila the Hun, the Mongolian conqueror. Those watching Mother Teresa had an increase in immune function. This was true even for those subjects who thought Mother Teresa was a fake. Those who had to endure the Attila the Hun film showed a decrease in immune function.

A study of coronary care patients found that intercessory prayer may have played a role in how well patients responded to treatment. Those patients who had been prayed for recovered better and experienced fewer complications than the patients who had not been prayed for. The results were statistically significant even though no one, except those who prayed, knew which patients were being prayed for.

While there are no well-controlled studies to provide evidence of a direct connection between spirituality, stress management and health, we can make some valuable inferences from related work. Let's look at the concept of spirituality as it relates to current research findings. I define spirituality as an individual's relationship with self, others, the natural world and a Divine power.

Studies related to stress hardiness show that the three characteristics—challenge, commitment and control—as well as social support were significant factors in determining whether subjects remained healthy. In this context, challenge, commitment and control can be considered part of our relationship with ourselves, that is, confidence in our ability to look at situations as opportunities for growth, belief in our ability to influence the events in our lives and the capacity to find meaning in our lives. In the same way, we can make the connection that social support reflects spirituality based on our relationship with others.

Medical sociologist Aaron Antonovsky developed a similar idea to explain why some women continued to be relatively healthy and happy despite having endured the atrocities of Nazi concentration camps in World War II. He defined his concept as "a sense of coherence," which included the attributes of comprehensibility, manageability and meaningfulness. Comprehensibility means the ability to find some logic and consistency in the situation we find ourselves in. Manageability refers to our belief that we have the resources to cope with demands placed on us whether those resources are personal capabilities, reliance on others or on a Divine power. Meaningfulness relates to our belief that the challenges of life are worth the effort. These attributes are consistent with the components of stress hardiness and reflect each of the aspects of spirituality—our relationship with ourselves, others, the environment and with a power greater than ourselves.

Optimism and hope may be viewed as aspects of our relationship with ourselves and with a Divine power. People who are optimistic do not blame themselves or see themselves as flawed when troubles occur in their lives. People who are hopeful believe in their ability to face and overcome personal challenges. Optimism and hope have also been associated with the belief that there is meaning and order to life and that a higher power is watching over them.

Many other studies support the role of an individual's relationship to others as an important factor in the stress, illness and recovery process. These include research relating to heart disease, breast cancer, arthritis, chronic pain, AIDS and loneliness.

These aspects of spirituality—stress hardiness, coherence, self-efficacy, optimism, hope and social support—are all consistent with the definition of stress. People with these characteristics are more likely to view potential stressors as opportunities for growth rather than as threats. They are able to rely on these spiritual attributes as a means of increasing their positive perception and ability to cope with the situations they find themselves in. As a result, their experience of stress may be less intense or they may be less likely to experience stress at all. In either case, research tells us that in the face of stress, these attributes may act as a buffer to protect the immune system.

While recognizing the absence of scientific proof, such well-known researchers as Jon Kabat-Zinn, Joan Borysenko, Herbert Benson and Dean Ornish believe in the importance of spirituality based on their observations of the subjects who participate in their studies. Dr. Ornish offers this insight: "I see in almost every heart patient a sense of isolation, of not having or being enough. I've become increasingly convinced that we are dealing here with emotional and spiritual dimensions." Long a proponent of what he calls the "Faith Factor," Dr. Benson and his colleagues have found that relaxation training or the "relaxation response," as he refers to it, is conncected with a greater sense of spirituality as measured by test scores. People who reported an increased sense of spirituality, i.e., the presence of an energy, a force, a Divine power that was beyond themselves, also noted the greatest medical benefits as compared to those who did not have this experience.

Treating the Mind and Body as One

Though researchers are just beginning to evaluate the effectiveness of mind/body/spirit treatment strategies, findings to date are very supportive and encouraging. Some studies focus on single-method interventions, such as group therapy or meditation, while others focus on a combination of techniques. The more thoroughly tested approaches include relaxation training, meditation, biofeedback, hypnosis, guided imagery, group therapy, behavior modification, cognitive restructuring and individual psychotherapy. People who participate in these programs also receive conventional medical treatment. While more studies are needed, early work in this area provides a strong basis of support for using a holistic approach to stress management, particularly for stress-related symptoms and illnesses. Mind/body strategies are now offered at many hospitals and clinics around the country as well as at such leading medical schools as Harvard, Yale, Stanford and UCLA, which now have departments devoted to mind/body medicine.

Meditation and Relaxation Training

Dr. Herbert Benson, a Harvard cardiologist, was the first to document the physiological effects of meditation and its benefits in alleviating the stress response. In a study conducted in 1975 he found that subjects practicing Transcendental Meditation showed decreases in metabolism, heart rate, blood pressure, breathing rate, brain waves, blood lactate and muscle tension. Since then over 2,000 studies have shown that various relaxation techniques produce similar physiological results. Benson now uses a form of meditation he terms the "relaxation response" as the basis for his mind/body research and treatment of patients with a variety of physical symptoms. He currently heads the Mind/Body Medical Institute at New England Deaconess Hospital and Harvard Medical School, where programs are offered for hypertension, chronic pain, general stress-related symptoms, cancer, HIV+ disease, infertility, cardiovascular disease, insomnia, premenstrual symptoms and menopause. Programs include a combination of meditation, cognitive therapy, exercise and nutrition.

The Stress Reduction Clinic at the University of Massachusetts Medical Center, founded in 1979 by Jon Kabat-Zinn, Ph.D., also offers a mind/body program based on meditation and mindfulness. Participants with many different illnesses come together as a group for eight weeks of classes to learn meditation, yoga and breathing. Results from studies conducted at the clinic show that, over the length of the course, patients report a significant drop in the number of medical symptoms and psychological problems such as anxiety, depression and hostility. Patients also experience improvements in health-related attitudes and behaviors, and in how they view themselves and the world. These positive outcomes have been maintained for up to four years following participation in the program.

Guided Imagery

Stephanie and Carl Simonton began using a holistic approach to cancer treatment in the early 1970s. A key component of their program centers on the use of positive mental imagery. Mental imagery involves visualizing successful cancer treatment, healthy body functioning and attaining personal goals. Other components of the program include exercise, nutrition and positive attitude training. A report published by the Simontons in 1978 showed highly significant results for their patients who had originally been diagnosed with incurable malignancy. The Simontons' patients, on average, lived twice as long as those receiving medical treatment alone.

In a study of geriatric subjects, other researchers have found a connection between improved immune function and guided imagery. Those subjects who were taught progressive relaxation and guided imagery showed an increase in immune system cell activity and increased control of the immune system over the herpes virus. Subjects also reported health improvements.

Group Support

In Dr. David Spiegel's study of women with breast cancer (discussed in Chapter 5), group support was not only associated with increased survival rates but with other important benefits as well. It was found to significantly improve participants' coping skills and self-esteem and to reduce anxiety and depression.

Many other studies have since shown the positive influence of group support for cancer patients, not only in terms of survival time but also in terms of quality of life. The benefits of group support have also been widely reported in the treatment of illnesses ranging from arthritis and chronic pain to heart disease and AIDS.

Self-Efficacy

A study of arthritis patients participating in an arthritis self-management program showed that perceived self-efficacy was significantly correlated with symptom improvements. Remember that self-efficacy refers to a person's belief that he can achieve a specific goal or master a challenge. Results also showed a 20-percent reduction in pain, a 15-percent reduction in depression, a 40-percent reduction in doctor visits and a 20-percent increase in perceived self-efficacy. Program components included medical and treatment information, therapeutic exercise, relaxation techniques, nutrition and information about the interrelationship between stress, pain and depression. Participants were also taught coping and anxiety management skills and were encouraged to set their own achievable goals.

Cognitive Therapy

Still other studies show that cognitive therapy, developed by Aaron Beck, is an effective treatment for a variety of psychological disorders, particularly depression and anxiety. The relevance of cognitive therapy lies in its ability to promote optimism by working with clients at the level of their thoughts, feelings and core beliefs. A critical aspect of the therapy is helping clients to first become aware of how their thinking may be distorted, and then to replace distorted thinking with more objective and optimistic thoughts. Just as important, if not more so, cognitive therapy has been found to be as effective as antidepressant and anti-anxiety medication. As an example, when medication is prescribed for generalized anxiety and/or panic attacks without psychotherapy, 70 to 90 percent will relapse with more severe episodes within two months. In contrast, Beck, Emery and Greenberg report findings in their 1985 book, *Anxiety and Phobias: A Cognitive Approach*, showing that cognitive therapy alone, without drug treatment, has shown relapse rates as low as 0 percent after two years.

Multidimensional Holistic Approaches

A holistic stress management approach to treat heart disease has proven successful in not only stopping the progression of the disease but in actually reversing the disease process. Dean Ornish proved this with a study that followed two matched groups with severe heart disease. The control group followed traditional medical protocol that included 30 percent dietary fat intake, moderate exercise and no smoking. Another group followed Ornish's program of 10 percent dietary fat intake, no smoking, no stimulants, yoga, meditation, breathing, visualization, walking and group support. One year later, the control group was measurably worse, showing increased artery blockage. Ornish's group, on the other hand, began to show improvement within the first week of the study, and, at year end, 82 percent of the subjects had an average of 5.3 percent reduction in artery blockage. His program is now being used by hospitals across the country.

Michael Antoni and his colleagues have also applied a holistic stress management approach to the treatment of HIV infection with good results. Gay men in Antoni's study were divided into two groups. One group underwent a 10-week stress management program. The other group did not. Both groups were told that they would be given an AIDS test five weeks into the study. Psychological and immune function tests were administered three days before and one week after the men were given the results of their tests. HIV-positive subjects who had undergone stress management training showed little or no change in anxiety or depression and showed an increase in immune function, as compared to HIV-positive subjects in the control group. Those in the control group showed significant increases in depression and anxiety and a drop in immune function. Researchers followed up with the HIV-positive subjects from both groups two years later. They found that those who had continued to practice stress management techniques were more likely to have higher immune function and less likely to have developed full-blown AIDS than those who did not practice stress management techniques. The results of the study show that practicing stress management techniques has positive effects on psychological and immune system functions both during an acute stressor (being told of HIV status) and for significant time periods afterwards. Antoni's stress management program included group support, emotional expression, cognitive restructuring, assertiveness training, stress education, breathing, relaxation training and guided imagery.

Although research findings to date provide convincing evidence that the mind and body are intimately connected and that stress plays a crucial role in this connection, more work needs to be done to fully understand these interrelationships. More comprehensive studies are needed that control specifically for each component linked to the mind/body connection. Be aware that preliminary findings must not be taken out of context or exaggerated in terms of identifying a single "cure" for a particular illness. Care also must be taken not to turn evidence of the psychological components of physical health or disease into another reason for self-blame when illness occurs.

Researchers are still gathering data to help us understand the complexities of the mind/body connection. However, what is abundantly clear from PNI studies thus far is that it *is* possible to positively affect the state of our health and sense of well-being. Moreover, the stress management techniques and strategies that have been proven effective can be undertaken at relatively low risk and low cost to the individual.

The Physical Connection

The mind/body connection is easily demonstrated by the following exercise:

> Take a moment to close your eyes and imagine a shiny, ripe, yellow lemon. Now, picture taking a knife and cutting a slice of that lemon, smelling its citrus aroma as you do. Next, imagine taking that slice of lemon, bringing it to your lips and sucking the juice from it.

Most people will react to this mind/body connection "test" by experiencing a sour sensation, grimacing and perhaps even salivating more. Since the mind and body are intimately connected, the body responds to the imagery of the lemon as if it were a real experience. The body responds to the mind's messages, both in thought and image form, based on its prior experience and knowledge of lemons.

The critical importance of this mind/body connection becomes clear when we examine and understand the effects of stress on our health and well-being. Physiologically, the function of the stress response—known as the fight or flight response—was to equip prehistoric people with a mechanism to defend themselves against real physical dangers like saber-toothed tigers or dinosaurs. Fortunately, most of our physical threats are not so ominous

Dominick's

Dominick's

Enter for your chance to

WIN

a grand prize of one of two
2011 Ford Explorer XTL SUVs!

OTHER PRIZES INCLUDE $100 & $50 DOMINICK'S GIFT CARDS.

Here's how it works: LIMIT FOUR (4) CODES PER FRESH VALUES CARD HOLDER. Every time you accumulate $85*
in grocery purchases, you will receive a code to use on Dominicks.com to enter for your chance to win!

Enter this Code: **HQCKPK6VUR**

85 years
SWEEPSTAKES

41350 41129 11237
0976 4210 0032

today. Modern-day physical stressors that trigger the stress response might include:

○ Having a near-collision on the highway.
○ Encountering a fiercely barking rottweiler on your morning run.

Both situations can be considered episodic occurrences of stress—intermittent and of short duration. In such instances, the stress response is triggered by a thought about the potential stressor. In the first example, the potential stressor is visual. You notice that the brake lights of the car in front of you have been turned on. Your thought might be, "I have only moments to step on the brakes to stop my car or I will hit the car in front of me." Your mind and body then work together in the stress response to allow you to defend yourself by taking action. Here, the action is mobilizing your leg and arm muscles quickly to control the car. In the second example, your thought might be "Rottweilers are dangerous; this dog is going to hurt me." Here again, your mind and body work together to prepare you to fight off or run from the rottweiler.

Both scenarios represent situations that make appropriate use of the stress response. The mind and body are propelled to take short-term physical action. By slamming on the brakes, the body can use up the powerful hormones released during the stress response. In the second example, if the dog's owner came to your rescue and controlled the dog (without your having to flee or defend yourself), the stress hormones would remain in your bloodstream for a time before being reabsorbed. In both examples, the body is wonderfully engineered to withstand these brief, momentary episodes of stress and returns to balance or homeostasis relatively quickly.

Most of our threats, however, come not as real, but as perceived threats usually to our emotional equilibrium. In such cases, there often is no appropriate physical action the body can take to make use of the stress hormones that are released in response to this perceived threat. Examples of such episodic stressors that might trigger the stress response are:

o   Your boss asks you into her office for a meeting.
o   Your spouse or child is late coming home.

These situations are not stressful in and of themselves. It is the meaning we assign to them that turns them into stressors. When your boss asks you to come to her office, you may begin to think threatening thoughts such as: "She didn't like that report I did, I should have spent more time on it, I can't handle the humiliation of making a mistake." When your spouse or child is late, you may begin to worry that something horrible has happened to them. Thoughts such as these can trigger the stress response and, though no physical action is taken, the body can usually recover relatively easily from these types of occasional stressful episodes.

However, if the stress response is triggered often enough because of perceived threats to our emotional well-being and no physical action is taken, the stress response can be chronically activated and eventually harm the body. The body's defense mechanisms become worn down, resulting in a variety of stress symptoms and illness. The following are examples of stressors that might trigger chronic stimulation of the stress response:

1. Ellen is the branch manager of a bank that is downsizing. She and the other employees have not received raises in several years, vacant positions are not being filled and layoffs have been occurring regularly. Ellen is responsible for making sure that the same amount of work gets done with fewer people. She is also responsible for selecting and informing employees about layoffs. Money is tight so Ellen and her husband both need to work to pay the bills. They also need health coverage for their son, who was born with several birth defects, which left him physically and mentally handicapped.

After working 40 hours a week, doing daily physical therapy with her son and otherwise maintaining a household, Ellen takes little time for herself. She is experiencing a great deal of stress and stress-related symptoms such as sleeplessness, racing thoughts, grinding teeth, anxiety, gastrointestinal problems and an inability to concentrate. Some of the thoughts that create stress for her are: "I could be laid off at any time. I couldn't cope with the loss of money and health benefits. If only I could work harder and get this place running more efficiently, we wouldn't have to lay off any more people. The employees blame me for the layoffs. I cannot waste time doing things for myself because my husband's and child's needs are more important than mine."

2. John works for a large government contract shipbuilding company that receives most of its work through federal government contracts. He is currently the only radiographer at the work site. Another radiography position was left vacant a year ago. At certain stages in the shipbuilding process, John must approve radiographic film before the next stage can begin. Because John is trying to do the work of two people, there is always a backlog. To complicate matters, John often has to reject film because of poor quality, and this delays progress even further. John's company has been on a six-day work week for the past nine months, and John has not taken a day off in twelve months. In his spare time, he is doing most of the construction work for an addition on his home.

Recently, John has been experiencing periods of high anxiety and panic, racing and negative thoughts, shortness of breath and heart palpitations. His doctor has ruled out coronary and cardiovascular abnormalities. Some of John's stressful thoughts are: "If I don't get all this work done, I'll be fired. If I don't get all this work done on time, I will be personally responsible for slowing production and bringing the contract in late, which will jeopardize the company's ability to get more contracts. The other workers are purposely bringing me bad film because they don't like me. They are trying to make my job more difficult. If I take a vacation or even a day off, my job will be in jeopardy. I don't have the right to take time off with all this work to be done. But I also need to work on the addition because we need the room and, if I do it myself, we'll save money."

3. Marie is married to her second husband and has custody of her three children from her previous marriage. She is a former teacher and is now a full-time homemaker. Her days are filled with grocery shopping, preparing meals, driving the kids to and from doctors' appointments and after-school activities, and cleaning the house. She is also responsible for arranging and supervising the work being done on refurbishing their home. Somehow, she also finds time to volunteer for civic and church organizations. Marie and her husband rarely take time for them-

selves. They are determined to make sure the kids come first and that endless household projects get done. Marie continues to have conflicts with her ex-husband over child-rearing responsibilities and financial child support.

For a long time, Marie has felt tired, anxious and depressed. Nonetheless, she continues her hectic pace. Her muscles are tense and she has had frequent, lingering colds. Some of her stressful thoughts are: "Since I don't have a job and I am just a homemaker, I should be able to take care of the house, the kids, my husband and volunteer work with no problem. I am embarrassed to tell people that I am just a homemaker because they will think less of me. My ex-husband will do anything to make my life miserable. I don't deserve to take time for myself or with my husband if the house isn't taken care of. I don't deserve to feel depressed. I have everything anyone could want."

The effects of emotional stress are evident in each of these examples. To truly appreciate its pervasiveness, it is important to understand the underlying physical functions and processes involved in the stress response. At one time or another, every system in the body becomes involved in the stress response, beginning with the central nervous system (CNS) and including the autonomic nervous system (ANS), the endocrine system and the immune system. Let's take a close look at the physiological reactions involved in the stress response.

Episodic stress

1. A message from one of the senses (sight, sound, smell, touch or taste) stimulates the brain's reticular activating system (RAS), which filters information to decide whether the stimulus is important. For example, someone who lives near railroad tracks is probably used to hearing the train go by. On the other hand, someone visiting would most likely not be used to hearing the sound. This person's RAS would filter this sensory stimulus as new and important information that could be a potential stressor.

2. The RAS sends the message to the hypothalamus, instructing it to be on the alert for possible action. The message is also

sent to the cortex, informing it of an important stimulus (a potential stressor).

3. The cortex interprets the message from the RAS and provides cognitive interpretation about whether the stimulus is a threat or not.

4. The cortex sends the message back to the hypothalamus, which integrates this cognitive message with emotional content from the limbic system to begin activation of the stress response. The neurological connection between the cortex, the limbic system and the hypothalamus provides the mechanism for how thoughts and emotions play a role in the stress response.

5. If safety is perceived, the stress response is turned off. The body returns to its resting state.

6. If a threat is perceived, the hypothalamus stimulates activation of the adrenal glands.

7. The adrenal glands are made up of two components, the adrenal medulla and the adrenal cortex. The hypothalamus stimulates the adrenal medulla via electrochemical impulses and stimulates the adrenal cortex via the pituitary, which releases the hormone ACTH into the bloodstream.

8. Once stimulated, the adrenal medulla releases epinephrine (adrenaline) and other hormones that affect the cardiovascular system by increasing heart rate and metabolism and constricting blood vessels.

9. When the adrenal cortex is stimulated, it discharges cortisol, which increases energy in the body by releasing glucose, fatty acids and amino acids (protein) from cells and organs into the bloodstream. Aldosterone also is discharged, which increases energy by retaining sodium (salt), which in turn increases blood pressure, blood volume and the amount of blood being pumped through the heart.

10. If the stress response results in physical action (fight or flight), the body can expend the energy created by the stress response and then return to homeostasis or balance.

Chronic stress

1. If the stress response continues or is repeated often enough, the body is not able to expend the energy it creates by taking physical action. The stress hormones therefore remain circulating in the system, and the body continues to be alarmed.

2. Under these conditions, the RAS may adapt to frequent stress stimulation by staying stimulated.

3. After repeated or ongoing activation of the stress response, natural energy stores of glucose, fatty acids and amino acids (protein) become depleted.

4. Without adequate protein supplies, the immune system's ability to produce white blood cells and virus-fighting antibodies is impaired, leaving the body susceptible to disease.

5. If fatty acids continue to be released into the bloodstream as part of the stress response, they promote the formation of plaque in the arteries that leads to atherosclerosis.

6. If salt retention continues as part of the stress response, the resulting increase in blood pressure jeopardizes the cardiovascular system.

7. If the above biological responses continue, the body attempts to adapt with a mechanism known as the general adaptation syndrome (GAS) or the biological stress syndrome. The GAS includes three stages: alarm, resistance and exhaustion. This adaptation is the reason disease may develop in response to stress.

8. During the alarm stage, all body systems are affected; however, no specific organ is affected more than any other.

9. During the resistance stage, the body attempts to protect itself from the life-threatening effects of repeated stress arousal by channeling the arousal response from the CNS and cardiovascular system into less critical systems such as the gastrointestinal and muscular systems. In this stage, the body may learn to channel all stress arousal to a particular system,

which may cause it to eventually wear down and become dysfunctional or diseased.

10. Diseases of adaptation that may occur in the resistance and exhaustion stages involve the muscles, the skin, the brain and the gastrointestinal, cardiovascular and immune systems. Continued stimulation of the muscles or a set of muscles can lead to headaches, backaches, muscle pulls and tears, spastic esophagus, spastic colon, asthma, difficulty swallowing, tightness in the chest, vision problems, TMJ and arthritis. Stomach functions also may be disrupted, causing ulcers and other digestive problems. Intestinal functions, too, can be affected, causing diarrhea or constipation. (A list of stress symptoms is provided on pages 72–73).

11. Once a particular system begins to break down, the body is in the exhaustion stage. It looks for another system to take over. As other systems become involved and break down, critical body functions become diminished and more life-threatening illnesses may occur, which may eventually lead to death.

12. Stress arousal causes increased activity in the brain, which creates beta waves, making an individual more susceptible to the effects of stress arousal. Repeated stress arousal can also disrupt the function and activity of the skin, resulting in eczema, psoriasis, hives or acne. In addition, it can cause a chronic increase in heart rate, high blood pressure and atherosclerosis that can lead to heart attack. Migraines also are a form of vascular irregularity. The immune system's response to stress includes disruption in the activity and production of disease-fighting immune cells. Diseases of the immune system include cancer, AIDS, rheumatoid arthritis and chronic respiratory conditions.

Since this book focuses on stress as it is triggered by our thoughts, it is also important to look specifically at what happens to our thought processes when we experience stress:

1. The adrenaline secreted during the stress response also acts to stimulate the RAS.

2. The RAS causes the neurons in the brain to fire two to three times faster than normal. When brain activity is increased in this way, it makes us think faster and causes our emotions to intensify.

3. The more threatening we perceive a stressor to be, the stronger the stress response is, creating greater stimulation of the RAS and a subsequent greater increase in brain activity.

4. When brain activity is increased in this way, our thoughts race and become fragmented. Memory and critical thinking abilities are impaired as a result, causing us to be impulsive or make irrational decisions that often lead to more stress.

Every negative thought we think produces a stress response in our bodies. The intensity of that response is determined by the degree to which we perceive that thought as a threat. Understanding this extensive and complex physical response to a single negative thought offers another compelling reason to be aware of and to honor the mind/body connection.

STRESS SYMPTOMS

Behavioral
Accident prone
Avoidance
Change in social
  habits
Changes in eating,
  drinking, smok-
  ing, taking
  medication
Chronic lateness
Fidgeting
Foot or finger
  tapping
Hyperventilation
Immobility
Impulsive behavior
Loss of interest in
  physical

appearance
Nightmares
Procrastination
Restlessness
Sexual difficulties/
  disinterest
Shallow breathing
Sighing
Sleep problems

Cognitive
Confusion
Daydreaming/
  dissociation
Distorted thinking
Easily distracted
Fearful thoughts
In a daze, haze, fog
Indecision

Loss of concentration
Loss of creative
  thinking
Loss of memory
Lost of objectivity/
  perspective
Negative thinking
Preoccupation
Racing thoughts

Emotional
Agitation
Alarm
Anger
Anxiousness
Depression
Fear/fright
Free-floating anxiety

Frustration
Guilt
Helplessness
Hopelessness
Impatience
Irritability
Jittery
Loss of control
Moodiness
Nervousness
Panic
Restlessness
Self-consciousness
Shakiness
Tension
Uneasiness
Worry

Cardiovascular
Chest pain
Cold hands and/or
  feet
Dizziness
Faintness
Heart palpitations
High blood pressure
Migraine headaches
Racing heartbeat
Sweaty palms/
  increased
  perspiration

Endocrine
Arthritic joint pain
Bloating/water
  retention

Changes in skin
  color/pallor
Diabetes
Excessive thirst
Fatigue
Infertility
Menstrual problems
Skin rashes/acne
Unusual changes in
  body temperature

Gastrointestinal
Abdominal pain
Acid stomach
Belching
Change in appetite
Constipation
Diarrhea
Gas
Gas pains/cramping
Heartburn
Intestinal pain
Nausea
Urination problems
Vomiting

Immune System
Allergies
Frequent flus/colds
Frequent infections
Herpes
Mononucleosis
Mouth sores
Strep throat

Muscular
Back pain

Clumsy movements
Facial pain
Frowning
Grinding/clenching
  teeth
Increased startle
  reaction
Jaw pain/ache
Muscle twitching/
  spasm
Muscular aches
Muscular weakness
Nervous tics
Pacing
Shaky/strained voice
Strained face
Tension headaches
Tight muscles
Trembling/shaking
Wobbly legs

Respiratory
Choking sensation
Lump in throat
Pressure in chest
Rapid breathing
Shallow breathing
Shortness of breath

Skin
Acne
Flushed face
Generalized sweating
Hives
Hot and cold spells
Itching
Pale face

The Role of Thoughts, Beliefs and Emotions

As discussed earlier, potential stressors do not trigger the stress response directly. Rather, it is the way we perceive a potential stressor at any given moment—either as a threat or an opportunity—that determines whether we experience stress or not. Perception, and therefore the experience of stress, is a function of our thoughts and beliefs. The strategies of cognitive therapy and rational emotive therapy are based on this premise and also on the assumption that most stressful thoughts are distorted and/or irrational.

According to cognitive theory, thoughts form the basis of our beliefs, which give rise to our emotions, which ultimately drive our behavior:

Thoughts & Beliefs → Emotions → Behaviors

Researchers in thought physiology have proven that every thought we think gets transferred to every cell in the body within milliseconds. From stress physiology, we've learned that the cortex (the thinking part of the brain) and the limbic system (the feeling part of the brain) are closely interconnected and contribute to the stress response. Given the interrelationship between thoughts and the stress response, combined with the speed at which thoughts are communicated within the body, it is essential to understand how thoughts, beliefs and emotions interact with potential stressors in triggering the stress response.

What are Thoughts?

Thoughts represent how we interpret information taken in by the senses. According to Jon Kabat-Zinn, "Thoughts dictate the way we perceive and explain our reality including our relationship with self, others and the world." In *Controlling Stress and Tension*, Daniel Girdano and his colleagues explain thoughts somewhat more broadly as

> . . . all complex interactions and transformations performed on the information taken in from the environment. Thought requires a store of information on the self, the environment and the interaction between the two. Thought process can be found in both the conscious awareness mode and the nonconscious, nonawareness mode.

Childhood Programming

Where does this store of information Girdano refers to come from? Researchers and theorists tell us that thoughts and beliefs are learned and that many of our thoughts and beliefs are the result of childhood programming. We use these thoughts and beliefs to interpret the experiences we have as well as the world we live in.

Often, what we think of as stress in the present can be connected to programmed beliefs from childhood. Nationally known theorist and counselor John Bradshaw postulates that by the time we reach the age of five we have been programmed with at least 20,000 hours of parental "tapes." These parental tapes include beliefs and attitudes concerning every aspect of our lives from how to think and feel, what type of partner to marry and what type of work to engage in, to how to communicate and express emotions. We receive additional "programs" from other important people in our lives including relatives, teachers, peers, religious and other authority figures. Often, these programs play over and over again in our minds like endless tape loops.

Self-Concept and Self-Esteem

Not surprisingly, parental messages and messages from other important people in our lives have a significant impact on the development of our self-concept. Self-concept is the image we hold of ourselves that is developed, in part, by evaluating input from those around us. Nathaniel Branden, often referred to as the "father of the concept of self-esteem" describes several components of self-concept including self-worth, self-love and self-esteem. In this context, self-worth refers to the belief that our basic worth as a person is equal to that of any other person and that we are worthy and deserving of happiness. Self-love refers to our ability to feel compassion for ourselves. Self-worth and self-love are considered to be inherent capacities that may be reduced or diminished through life experiences. Self-esteem refers to our belief that we can make competent and appropriate decisions about our lives. This belief is based on how we evaluate our actions.

Internal Validation/Listening to Your Inner Voice

Our ability to feel self-worth and self-love directly affects our self-esteem. To evaluate our actions positively, we must feel compassion for ourselves and feel worthy of the happiness that compassion brings. We are more likely to experience healthy self-esteem when we are able to validate our actions positively based on our internal set of values and beliefs, in other words, when approval and acceptance of self comes from within. This is often referred to as internal validation or as listening to our inner voice. When we listen to our inner voice, we are able to evaluate what is right for us by relying on our internally validated values and beliefs to trigger an emotional response which affirms or disaffirms our questions and concerns.

When we depend on the values and judgments of others to determine how we feel about ourselves, we are less likely to have healthy self-esteem. This is because we are relying on unpredictable variables such as the specific emotional and/or mental state of others on any given day and their own level of self-esteem. Looking outside to substantiate our self-esteem is called external validation. It often leads to insecurity and self-doubt.

Limits and Boundaries

The concept of limits and boundaries also relates to internal validation. It refers to our ability to rely on our own inner resources to make decisions for ourselves. In doing so, we learn to understand where we, as emotional and spiritual beings, end and others begin. Healthy limits and boundaries allow us to be in touch with our own inner resources and use them as a guide to determine what is right for us. Otherwise, we allow the feelings and circumstances of others to undermine our ability to take care of ourselves. In *Beyond Codependency*, Melodie Beattie describes limits and boundaries in terms of the borders which delineate our personal territory:

> Our boundaries define and surround all our energy, the individual self that we each call "me." There is a place where I end and you begin. Our goal is learning to identify and have respect for that line.

Codependency describes the condition of not being aware of, or exerting, our limits and boundaries. Charles Whitfield defines codependency as "any suffering and/or dysfunction that is associated with, or results from, focusing on the needs and behaviors of others." Codependency also involves a lack of internal validation and attempting to control what is not in our power to control—particularly the thoughts, feelings and behaviors of others.

Emotions

Thoughts and beliefs give rise to emotions, which are a combination of cognitive and physiological processes. Through our cognitive processes, we interpret internal or external input as either safe or dangerous. Depending on what we tell ourselves about ourselves and any person, event or circumstance we are dealing with, we experience fear, anger, sadness, happiness or other feelings in response.

Emotions are complicated events. Branden explained them in this way:

> An emotion is both a physical and mental event. It may be defined as an automatic psychological response involving both mental and physiological features, to our subconscious appraisal of what we perceive as the beneficial or harmful relationship of some aspect of reality to ourselves. Emotions reflect the perceiver's value response to different aspects of reality: "for me or against me," "good for me or harmful," "to be pursued or to be avoided" and so forth.

So we take in information from the senses and evaluate it in the thinking part of the brain (the cortex) in order to determine whether we are safe or whether we are being threatened in some way. This basic thought, that we are either safe or are being threatened, is then transferred to the feeling part of the brain (the limbic system), where emotional content is added to the process. Emotions are the way we prepare ourselves to react to conditions around us. Our emotions serve as the trigger for physiological responses that aid us in keeping safe and in balance. This cognitive-emotional-physiological process has a dual purpose. It tells us whether or not our needs are being met and tells us to take action to get our needs met and keep them met. Bradshaw describes emotions as

> . . . signals from the body telling us of a need, a loss, a satiation. The energy is used to help us act effectively to take care of ourselves. Emotions give important information about what we need to do, what we want or how we want to change.

Emotions generally can be categorized as anger, fear, sadness or happiness. The first three are most frequently associated with stress, particularly if we are unable to recognize them and process them in a healthy way. Fear and anger allow us to fight or run away to protect ourselves from perceived threat. Sadness allows us to go through a grief process to come to terms with and move beyond our losses. Happiness allows us to be aware that our needs are being met and to experience a sense of well-being and safety. If happiness is sustained for a period of time, it also allows us to experience inner peace.

Wilhelm Reich, the father of bioenergetics, discovered that repressing emotions yields a bodily response. This response involves muscular contraction, interrupted breathing leading to less available oxygen, and a diminished capacity to feel. Unless this tension is released, it stays stored in the body. In other words, repressing emotions is stressful to the body. If there is enough stored emotional tension, the body will begin to break down and experience stress symptoms and disease.

When Thoughts and Emotions are Stressful

As human beings, we require certain basic needs to be met to survive. Among these are food, shelter, safety, nurturing and unconditional love. The first three needs are obvious; they are all physical necessities for survival. The need for love and nurturing, however, may be less obvious, although it shouldn't be. Research shows that lack of nurturing and love can have serious physical effects. It can manifest itself as the "failure to thrive" syndrome or a form of psychological dwarfism in which a growth hormone ceases being produced in children who are not given enough affection. The emotional effects of inadequate love and nurturing also can have serious consequences, particularly with regard to stress.

As children, we are not able to meet our own basic physical needs so we rely on our parents to do so. As a result, we view our parents as all-powerful in their capacity to protect us and keep us safe. Bradshaw calls this the "deification" of our parents. Bradshaw, Branden and others theorize that children empower parents in this way to safeguard themselves from the anxiety of being dependent and helpless. This theory has an important corollary. If a parent is having a bad day and treats a child badly or if a parent is abusive emotionally, physically or sexually, the child is not developmentally able to understand that the parent is at fault. The child, therefore, internalizes the belief that he/she is at fault and is bad, wrong, unworthy and undeserving. Branden explains that when parents act badly all the child knows is that he is hurt. He describes the consequences of this hurt in the following way:

> To believe that their hurt bears no important relation to their own actions but is merely the end product of unsolved problems residing within their parents would only generate an intensified feeling of powerlessness. They can not solve their parents' problems. So what are they to do? At this point the need for intelligibility and the need for an experience of efficacy in effect conspire against the child. They often lead the child to a solution that yields short-term benefits while laying the foundation for a long-term disaster in which self-esteem turns against itself. . . . The solution consists of some variant of the idea "There's something wrong with me." "I'm undeserving, unloveable." The child tells himself, in effect: "It's too terrifying to imagine that my parents do not know what they are doing. I will disown what I see, repress what I feel—and take the guilt on myself and if I can please my parents then I will get the nurturing I crave."

Based on the work of developmental psychologist Jean Piaget, Bradshaw describes a child's thinking in this way:

> They [the parents] are gods, all-powerful, almighty and all-protecting. No harm can come to the child as long as he has parents. This magical idealization serves to protect the child from the terrors of the night, which are about abandonment and to the child, death. For example, if the parents are abusive and hurt the child through physical, sexual, emotional or mental pain, *the child will assume the blame, make himself bad, in order to keep the all-powerful protection against the terrors of the night*. For the child at this stage to realize the inadequacies of parents would produce unbearable anxiety. . . . No child, because of his helplessness, dependency and terror wants to accept the belief that his parents are inadequate, sick, crazy or otherwise imperfect. *To be safe and to survive, a child must idealize his parents and make himself bad*.

From this standpoint, a child also comes to accept and assimilate his parents' messages to him about himself and the world around him. He does this in an effort to gain the love and approval that he desires and needs. A child who experiences unconditional love, that is, love that is freely given regardless of the child's actions, behaviors or personal characteristics, receives a message that supports healthy self-love, self-worth and self-esteem. That basic message includes "I'm okay and I'm appropriate to the world." A child who experiences love based on any condition other than that he exists and is worthy of love, receives a message that undermines and erodes self-love, self-worth and self-esteem. That basic message includes "I'm not okay, there is something wrong with me." In Bradshaw's view, a child that is loved unconditionally learns that he is a human *being*—that he is worthy of love just by being. A child that is loved conditionally learns that he is a human *doing*—that he must try to earn love through his actions.

The degree to which a child absorbs these messages depends on many factors. Stress researchers and experts agree, however, that our self-concept directly affects our susceptibility to stress as well as the effect stress will have on us. Parents and other significant people in our lives convey messages to us both verbally and non-verbally. As children, we internalize negative messages about ourselves in any number of ways. In *Healing the Child Within*, Charles Whitfield offers descriptions of some of the more negative rules and negative messages we might hear as children:

Negative Rules

- Don't express your feelings.
- Don't get angry, upset, cry.
- Do as I say, not as I do.
- Avoid conflict.
- Don't ask questions.
- Don't discuss the family with outsiders.
- Be seen and not heard.
- Don't talk back.
- Don't contradict me.
- Always be in control.
- Always maintain the status quo.

Negative Messages

o   You're not good enough.
o   Your needs are not all right with me.
o   Big boys don't cry.
o   Act like a nice girl.
o   You're stupid, bad, selfish.
o   It's your fault.
o   You owe it to us.
o   I'm sacrificing myself for you.
o   We won't love you if you . . .
o   You'll never accomplish anything.
o   Be dependent.
o   We wanted a boy/girl.
o   I wish I never had you.

These negative messages are absorbed and internalized by the child and result in negative childhood programming which can take the form of negative or critical self-talk. As adults, we may become our own critical parent, replaying childhood messages over and over in situations which, consciously or unconsciously, remind us of similar circumstances from our childhood. For example, you might find yourself criticizing yourself for speaking up at a business meeting, saying things to yourself like: "Why did I say that? I sounded really stupid." Or you may not speak up because the critical voice cautions you: "What you have to say is not important, don't make a fool of yourself." You may hold this view because you were criticized for speaking up during family gatherings when you were young.

Negative self-talk is a reflection of our self-concept. The more we criticize and judge ourselves, the more we question our worthiness, our "okayness." The less loving we are toward ourselves, the less competent we feel as human beings. The lower our self-concept is the more likely we are to interpret situations and conditions as being dangerous to us and the more likely we are to experience stress. When we engage in negative self-talk, we are, in effect, triggering the stress response. We do this by telling ourselves that either something is a threat to us or that we are unable to cope with the circumstances.

This situation is exacerbated by the fact that many of us also are programmed to repress our emotions from an early age. The negative messages we receive about emotions during our formative years tell us that having or expressing certain emotions— like anger and sadness—are not acceptable. Statements such as "Good girls don't get angry" or "Big boys don't cry" perpetuate the notion that expressing emotions is bad. Other negative messages tell us it's better not to show our feelings. Messages that tell us we must always be in control, for example, imply that having or expressing emotions is being out of control.

Emotions provide critical feedback

If we are programmed not to express or even "own" our emotions, we lose a crucial tool to help us make our way in the world. Emotions represent our inherent feedback mechanism for safety and self-protection. They are our first line of defense in the world. They tell us whether our limits and boundaries are being honored or dishonored. If we are not in touch with our emotions and we are unable to recognize or be aware of our emotions as they occur, we are less capable of protecting ourselves and keeping ourselves safe. When our negative self-talk interferes with our emotional signals, we experience doubt about our ability to cope with what is happening to us, around us and within us. We are unable to experience the internal validation and safety that comes from listening to our inner voice, asking ourselves what is right for us and feeling confident in the answer.

Free-floating anxiety

In the absence of internal validation, we are at risk of experiencing what is known as free-floating anxiety. Free-floating anxiety is the sense that something bad is going to happen even when there is no evidence to substantiate such a belief. This feeling tends to come from past experiences, where our state of happiness was abruptly interrupted by an event or circumstance we experienced as stressful. For example, you may have been playing happily by yourself one day when your dad came home from work after a bad day and started yelling at you. Since you were unable to understand that his bad mood did not have to do with you but with him, you may have internalized this event to mean that it is not okay to feel happy. Other messages which can create free-floating anxiety include internalized beliefs such as "Nothing in life comes easily," "There's a price to pay for happiness," "Happiness doesn't last," "It's not okay to be happy when other people are sad (sick, poor, suffering, starving, etc.)"

Free-floating anxiety is similar to Branden's concept of happiness anxiety, which comes from not feeling worthy of happiness. If we do not feel worthy of happiness, then experiencing happiness can create tension or anxiety. We then engage in behaviors to avoid or stop feeling happy before tension or anxiety sets in. When we feel free-floating anxiety or happiness anxiety, we are always expecting something to undermine our sense of well-being and constantly experiencing the stress triggered by that threatening belief.

The Stress Response Profile

Once we understand how thoughts, beliefs and emotions can lead to stress, we can form a more complete picture of the stress response cycle. As we've seen, the experience of stress begins with a potential stressor—a condition, situation, event or person. When our senses perceive a potential stressor we make a decision about whether the stressor is an opportunity or a threat. When we interpret the stressor as a threat, this leads to an emotion, generally fear or anger. Our fear or anger signals the body to prepare to cope with the threat in some way. It stimulates the fight/flight or stress response, which readies the body to take action which may be a healthy or unhealthy behavior that we have developed over time as a means of coping with stress. Many people develop maladaptive coping behaviors. These can include "numbing ourselves" to our own emotions and needs by engaging in negative thinking or poor eating, drinking, smoking, sleeping, busyness or other habits.

The stress response profile looks like this:

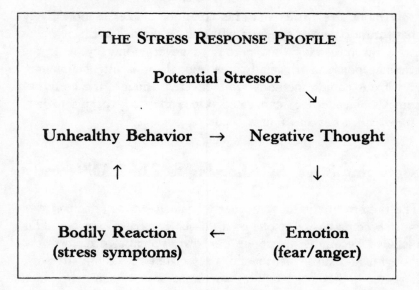

For example, your boss calls you in to his office for a meeting.

Potential Stressor	Boss asks for a meeting with you.
Negative Thought	"He didn't like the report I did and he's going to yell at me."
Emotion	Fear.
Bodily Reaction(s)	Sweaty palms, heart racing.
Unhealthy Behavior(s)	Avoid him, have a drink at lunch, start making excuses about the report before you know why he called you in.

If you always tell yourself negative thoughts about why the boss wants to talk to you even if there is no evidence that the reason is negative, your stress response may intensify. Your thoughts may become increasingly more negative, your fear may become stronger and your stress symptoms and unhealthy behaviors may become worse.

Each time the stress response is triggered without being managed in a healthy way, the mind and the body become increasingly more stress-reactive. This condition makes it more likely that future potential stressors will also be viewed as threats. The stress response may then become a never-ending cycle. If the stress response is triggered often enough or is intense enough, and if our coping methods are ineffective enough, the body becomes unbalanced or exhausted. Once the body begins to tire, stress symptoms and illness occur.

Managing Stress by Choosing to Think Differently

The bottom line is that in order to manage stress effectively we must become aware of our own unique response to stress. This includes becoming aware of our own potential stressors, the thoughts and subsequent feelings associated with those stressors, how our bodies react to the experience of stress and the kinds of behaviors we may engage in to cope with stress. Awareness is not enough, however. With this awareness we then have to commit ourselves to learning coping skills that can help us to prevent and reduce stress.

Since what we tell ourselves about a potential stressor is the key element in determining whether we experience stress or not, it is important to understand something about our thoughts. Just as thoughts can be learned, they can be unlearned. In fact, we can choose the way we think. If we can choose the way we think then we can choose the way we feel and behave. The strategies presented in Chapter 10 provide the groundwork for developing healthy coping mechanisms for dealing with our stressful thoughts, beliefs, emotions and behaviors.

Stress, Spirituality and Inner Peace

Managing stress involves more than learning to think differently, although that's a crucial first step. At the same time, there are certain spiritual attributes that make us resilient in the face of the negative effects of stress. We need to develop and enhance some of those attributes and explore our own spirituality in order to experience inner peace. First, let's review the broader concept of spirituality and consider its relationship to stress management.

Earlier, spirituality was defined as our relationship with ourselves, others and with all things in the universe, including a Divine source. Religion may be considered a bridge to spirituality, but it is not necessarily synonymous with, or even an exclusive means of, deepening our spirituality.

It has been said that, "We are not human beings having a spiritual experience; rather we are spiritual beings having a human experience." As spiritual beings, we simply need to be in touch with our capacities for compassion, empathy and love in order to experience our spirituality to its fullest extent. In allowing ourselves to feel compassion, empathy and love for ourselves we open the door to experiencing inner peace.

Spirituality is often associated with a feeling that we are not alone, that there is a sense of purpose in our lives and that there is a part of us, perhaps our soul, which never dies. This sense can give us a feeling of being connected with others, with everything in the universe and with something that transcends our humanness. To feel connected in this way requires us to be open to our ability to feel compassion, empathy and love for others.

The notion that all things are connected is now bolstered by scientific research in the field of quantum physics. Writers like Fritzof Capra and Gary Zukav have examined evidence from quantum physics that supports the hypothesis that no separate parts exist in the universe. Both describe research evidence derived from Bell's Theorem that implies that all parts of the universe are connected in an intimate and immediate way.

This sense of connectedness, oneness or peace is also found in moments when we experience total absorption in whatever we are doing. This can be any activity from listening to music or watching the movement of the ocean to receiving or giving unconditional love. During these moments our awareness is fully in the present moment. We are not caught up in guilt feelings about the past or worry feelings about the future. In these moments there is no stress or anxiety because we are not focused on being threatened in any way. We are focused on the beauty of the here and now. These moments are often called times of transcendence, joy or enlightenment. They can reveal hints to us of the connectedness of all things and of a power greater than ourselves.

That part of us which is connected to a power greater than ourselves is sometimes referred to as our "higher self," "inner voice," "inner wisdom" or intuition—that part of us that reflects the energy of a Divine source or higher power in us—the part that is "God-like." In *Listening: How to Increase Awareness of Your Inner Guide,* Lee Coit describes our inner voice as a "power in us which is of God [that] gives us strength, vision, success, and peace." For many, it is an "Aha!" experience, a gut feeling or a sense of a light coming on. This is often accompanied by a calm, peaceful feeling as we experience a sense of inner knowing about thoughts, decisions or actions that are right for us.

Looking inside for answers instead of outside to the many competing influences in our lives allows us the opportunity to rely on our inner voice, gut instinct or intuition. In this way we are much less likely to experience the stress of sorting through our negative judgments, constricting "shoulds" and other people's agendas for us—all of which often get in the way. Ultimately, relying on our inner voice brings with it a sense of safety. This sense of safety arises from the knowingness that we always have this inner resource to guide us.

When we are in touch with our inner voice or our inner wisdom we feel safe enough to experience inner peace. Safety and inner peace begin to emerge when we can accept ourselves in the present moment, with compassion. Part of this compassion comes from accepting ourselves without self-criticism, self-evaluation or self-judgment. Inner peace also involves a healthy balance between control and letting go. The Serenity Prayer describes this balance, as the ability "to accept the things I cannot change, the courage to change the things I can and the wisdom to know the difference." When we achieve such balance, we also gain the ability to see potential stressors as opportunities rather than as threats, based on our sense of self-efficacy and self-esteem.

Wayne Muller, in *Legacy of the Heart*, describes inner peace in terms of the Buddhist concept of equanimity:

> Equanimity is the ability to experience the changes in our lives, circumstances, and feelings and still remain calm, centered, and unmoved. . . . As we cultivate equanimity within ourselves, we learn to be more like the mountain, finding that place of strength and courage within ourselves that enables us to withstand the slings and arrows of being human without being overwhelmed by fear.

Inner peace is an integral part of spirituality because when we experience it we accept ourselves in a loving way. Since it is almost impossible to give love or receive love from others without first being able to accept and love ourselves, our capacity for inner peace affects our relationships with others and with a power greater than ourselves. Therefore, developing a sense of connectedness that leads to inner peace begins when we accept ourselves with compassion.

The Dalai Lama, in accepting the Nobel Peace Prize, described the essence and the promise of inner peace:

> The question of real, lasting world peace concerns human beings, so basic human feelings are also at its roots. Through inner peace, genuine world peace can be achieved. In this, the importance of individual responsibility is quite clear. An atmosphere of peace must first be created within ourselves, then gradually expanded to include our families, our communities, and ultimately the whole planet.

One of the biggest stumbling blocks to letting our spirituality flourish and to experiencing inner peace comes from ignoring one of the most critical relationships we have—our relationship with ourselves. So much of our pain and suffering comes from feeling unworthy and undeserving of love. We cannot feel love and compassion for ourselves when we are beating ourselves up emotionally with distorted criticisms and judgments. This kind of self-abuse leads us to doubt our ability to cope with what life presents us. The more we feel threatened in this way, the more we experience stress.

If, in our relationship with ourselves, we do not treat ourselves with dignity and respect because we feel unworthy, undeserving or "less than," then we are not loving ourselves. We lack a spiritual connection with ourselves and therefore lack that sense of inner peace. On the other hand, when we are able to adopt an attitude of self-awareness and self-acceptance to quiet our minds and bodies and focus on the present moment, we are more likely to be in touch with our higher self and to experience inner peace.

For those who believe that we are created by and connected to a Divine source and that Divine source loves us unconditionally, it is somewhat easier to learn to treat ourselves with love and compassion. As we focus on ourselves as being made "in the image of God" and having "God in us" we can learn to love ourselves as our Divine power loves us and to treat ourselves with the same dignity and respect that our Divine power has for us.

When we learn to manage stress by developing and relying on our spiritual attributes and sense of spirituality, then preventing and managing stress comes from a much deeper place inside of us. When we have a strong sense of self-love, compassion and acceptance, when we have a sense of meaning and purpose in life, when we feel the safety that comes from listening to our inner voice, when we feel connected to others and a Divine Power, we are practicing the ultimate stress management strategies. Nurturing these qualities in ourselves provides the breeding ground for developing the attributes that keep us stress-resilient. They make it possible for us to release fear and, in doing so, to view stressors as opportunities for growth and learning as we trust in our ability to cope with whatever life presents us.

10

Do It Now!
Strategies for Relieving Stress

It is not enough to read about strategies and have knowledge about them, you must practice them and use them inorder for them to be effective.

Remember, the times when we need stress management strategies the most are the times when we are least likely to be able to use them—*unless* we have already practiced them thoroughly and made them an important part of our repertoire of coping skills. Too often we look for change without making an effort. The traditional medical model has taught us to rely on a pill or a procedure to make us well rather than to use our own personal power as an adjunct to treatment. Once you have mastered a few stress management strategies you will begin to feel more of your personal power. Having a sense of your personal power will motivate you to continue learning more strategies. It does not have to be difficult if you focus on the ultimate reward of bringing more health and inner peace into your life.

* * *

I recommend the following Daily Program to each of my clients as a means of jump-starting them into managing their stress:

How to Begin: Daily Program

○ Begin each day with the Peaceful Wake-Up Call (See page 98).
○ Breathe deeply every hour for one to three minutes while doing a mini Mind/Body Check and repeating appropriate affirmations.
○ Develop three or four affirmations to be used with your hourly breathing routine. Consider affirmations about:

1. A specific stress management goal you may have at the moment, such as, "My mind, my body, and my emotions are at peace" or, "I feel calm and centered."

2. Your relationship with yourself such as "I am as compassionate with myself as I am with other people," or, "I accept myself in this present moment without judgment, evaluation or criticism."

3. Your relationship with a Divine power: "God loves me".

4. Your long-term goals: "I am creating everything I need for my emotional, physical and spiritual well-being."

○ Do some form of meditation/relaxation training once a day.
○ Whenever you feel anxious, stressed or uncomfortable, use the Self-Reflection Tool (See page 129).
○ Develop a regular exercise routine.
○ Pay attention to how you are feeding your body. Develop a healthy nutrition regimen.
○ End the day the way you started, adapting the Peaceful Wake-Up Call to create an evening ritual before sleep.

STRATEGIES

Read through the strategies once in order to familiarize yourself with them. You will find strategies for your mind, including cognitive and emotional strategies, strategies for your body and strategies for spiritual development. Any strategy which helps to improve the quality of your relationship with yourself, others and a power greater than yourself can be considered a spiritual strategy. Many of the strategies described here are designed to do just that.

If there is a strategy that seems particularly appropriate to your life right now, start working with it. Otherwise you might want to start working with two or three strategies a week until you feel comfortable that they are working effectively for you, then move on to other strategies.

Try not to get overwhelmed by all the material that follows. Used appropriately, these are the most powerful and empowering strategies to start with:

o   Healing Breath Work.
o   Peaceful Wake-Up Call.
o   Meditation/Relaxation. Choose one method or try different methods until you feel comfortable with one. Many people find it easy to start with a guided meditation or relaxation exercise on tape. See page 200 to order my tape.
o   Mind/Body Checks.
o   Identifying Negative Self-Talk.
o   Recognizing Distorted Thinking.
o   Eliminating Negative Self-Talk and Distorted Thinking.
o   Evaluating and Eliminating the Shoulds.
o   Affirmations.
o   Self-Reflection Tool.

Healing Breath Work

The breath is the anchor point for stress management. Breathing is the one stress management tool we have available to us at every moment, no matter how intense our stress experience is. Once learned, healing breath work does not require special preparation, circumstances or equipment. In fact, using the breath properly may be the single, most elegant technique to facilitate emotional and physical relaxation. Through the use of healing breath work we can interrupt the stress response, trigger the flow of relaxing endorphins, become aware of our stressful thoughts and make a conscious decision to choose a healthy response to potential stressors.

The purpose of breathing is to allow the red corpuscles in the blood to energize the body by picking up oxygen from the lungs and carrying it throughout the body to every cell, nerve, organ and muscle. Once the blood cells release oxygen they then pick up carbon dioxide which is the major waste of the body and transport it back to the lungs for the purpose of expelling it. The power and importance of proper breathing has been known to yoga practitioners for thousands of years. Students of yoga understand that the oxygen we take into our lungs provides us with our life force and that proper breathing energizes the body and detoxifies it. Proper breathing also improves the functioning of the organs (especially the heart) and all the bodily systems including the circulatory, nervous and digestive systems. Just as important, it calms the mind so we can experience inner peace.

Modern scientific research validates the fact that the way we breathe has a significant impact on our physical and psychological well-being. When we are feeling stressed or anxious, our breathing becomes irregular and shallow. We may find ourselves breathing too fast and/or holding our breath without even realizing it. When our breath is shallow we are filling only a small portion of our lungs with oxygen. The more we constrict our oxygen intake in this way the less energy and balance we provide to our bodies. Shallow breathing is often referred to as chest breathing, it moves an average of only 500 cubic centimeters of oxygen through our lungs. When we are breathing deeply, using our diaphragm muscle (diaphragmatic or abdominal breathing), we are able to move as much as 4,000 to 5,000 cubic centimeters of oxygen through our lungs.

Research confirms that diaphragmatic breathing decreases heart rate, metabolic rate, blood sugar levels, pulmonary stress, muscle tension and fatigue and the perception of pain. This type of proper breathing also helps normalize blood flow in the lungs, improves the return of blood to the heart, and increases the flow of blood and oxygen to the brain and heart as well as oxygenation of the tissues. Diaphragmatic breathing also has a number of psychological effects including the capability to increase ego strength, emotional stability, confidence, alertness and the perceived control over one's environment. It also decreases anxiety, phobic behavior, depression and psychosomatic illness. Chest breathing has the opposite effect, both physically and psychologically.

We take over 24,000 breaths a day. That means we have at least 24,000 opportunities to be conscious of our breathing pattern and to use our breath to manage stress. Unfortunately, most of us, unless properly trained, chest breathe nearly all of the time. And while it takes a firm commitment to change long-standing habits, the benefits of proper breathing are highly rewarding. In my experience, people can experience a noticeable reduction in their stress level within just a few days of practicing proper breathing.

STRATEGIES

Use the following exercise to become familiar and comfortable with the basics of proper breathing. Continued practice is required in order to train your body to make abdominal breathing a natural reflex. Keep in mind that the ultimate goal is to make a majority of your 24,000 daily breaths abdominal ones. For now however, practice as often as you can and consider focusing on various ways to remind yourself to breathe properly.

Three-part breath:

You may try this exercise either sitting or lying down; or try it both ways to see which way is best for you. You may experience awkwardness at first as you get used to the rhythm, but this will disappear with practice.

1. Inhale slowly and as completely as possible as you expand first the belly (below the navel), then the diaphragm and finally the chest.

2. Hold for a few moments before exhaling.

3. Exhale in reverse pattern, slowly emptying the chest, diaphragm and then the belly.

4. Hold for a few moments before inhaling again.

5. Make sure that you exhale as fully and completely as you inhale.

6. Repeat 10 times the first few times you practice and then build up to a point where you feel comfortable with the process.

7. If you find yourself feeling stressed or anxious, continue to breathe like this until you feel more in control or more relaxed. If, at any time, you begin to feel stressed again just start your breathing technique and remember how much more in control and relaxed it makes you feel.

Tuning in to the breath

Healing breath work heightens awareness and encourages the release of tension that builds up so easily in the course of a day. Try healing breath work in the various circumstances you find yourself in during the day—in the morning before you get out of bed or when you are in the shower, during breaks at work, sitting in the car, sitting at your desk. You might also consider reminding yourself to practice healing breath work, particularly if you find yourself feeling stressed or anxious, as you prepare for work, get the kids ready for school, drive to or from work, wait in line or in traffic, before you start a new task, before you talk to someone who is a potential stressor, etc. Program your computer's screen saver to read "Breathe!" Some people also find it useful to put post-its or small colored dots in places like the bathroom, on the refrigerator, on the car dashboard or on the telephone to remind them to practice conscious breathing.

Using the breath to choose healthy responses to stress

So much of what we do during the day is automatic. In the same way, many of the coping mechanisms we use to manage stress are automatic and, as such, they may not be the most healthy responses for us. Take any and every opportunity you can to pause, breathe, become aware of what you are doing or what you are about to do and choose a healthy response. Allow the breath to create a moment in time to interrupt what might be unhealthy, automatic responses to potential stressors. For example, instead of lighting up a cigarette or eating or drinking something that is unhealthy for you, take a moment to pause, breathe, become aware and consciously choose your response. Then, eat a piece of fruit, drink a cup of herbal tea or spend three minutes doing healing breath work.

For people who have a hard time saying "no" to others it is helpful to take a moment to pause whenever anyone asks you to do something and then allow yourself to breathe, become aware of whether you really want to do what is being asked of you and choose the response that honors how you feel. Using the ringing of the telephone as a trigger for this technique can also be helpful. Whenever the telephone rings, remind yourself that you have at least three rings before the answering machine clicks on. Take this time to pause and breathe several times, mentally preparing yourself to be aware of what the person may be asking of you and how that will affect you so that you will be able to consciously choose the response that is best for you. For example, suppose you are having a busy week and a friend calls to ask you to lunch. Ordinarily you would automatically answer yes and then either feel stressed by the time pressure or spend time thinking of an excuse to cancel. Instead, take a moment to pause, breathe, become aware of your busy schedule and choose to say no. It only takes seconds to do this once you practice it a few times.

Peaceful Wake-Up Call

Are you the type of person who gets up in the morning, stumbles into the shower and then blindly heads toward the coffee maker in search of a jump start to the morning? Instead of relying on your first cup of coffee or tea to get your day started, why not try a more conscious, more peaceful approach?

I suggest creating a morning wake-up ritual to guide you into your day with a sense of appreciation, compassion and peace. This kind of ritual is also a useful tool for centering yourself. I guarantee this will not only reduce the stress of how you begin the day but will also set the tone to reduce stress all day long.

STRATEGY

Each morning when you wake up . . .

○ Take a few moments to become aware of your breathing, practicing a few diaphragmatic breaths.

○ As you do this, bring your attention to each part of your body, consciously moving from your toes up to your forehead.

○ Repeat any affirmations you may be working on. (See page 122.)

○ Then set your intention for the day. You can do this in many ways, for example, saying a prayer, a verse or a phrase that has meaning for you. One of my favorite verses was written by Thich Nhat Hanh, a Vietnamese Buddhist monk:

Waking up this morning, I smile. Twenty-four brand-new hours are before me. I vow to live fully in each moment and to look at all beings with eyes of compassion.

Make a special effort to say your personal prayer or verse with meaning and expression no matter how many times you have repeated it before. Smile as you are saying it, even if the best you can muster is to simply curl up your lips. It will change the chemistry in your body and make you feel lighter.

○ Next, take a few moments to focus on what you have to be grateful for. If you have trouble finding a place to start, begin with your ability to see, hear, touch, taste, smell, walk and talk, and move on from there. Try thinking of one thing you've never thought of before to be grateful for.

○ Finally, if you're comfortable with this, you can bring your attention to your connection with a power greater than yourself. There are countless ways to do this. You might try simply focusing on the words, "God (insert your own word for God) loves me unconditionally." If you have a hard time feeling this connection use this as an opportunity to add dimension and depth to your connection with the Divine. You can also visualize this connection by focusing on a beam of loving energy flowing from your heart to God (or your image of the Divine) and from God to you.

All of this takes as little as five to ten minutes! So even if you have young children or a hectic schedule, waking up five minutes earlier is not a major demand on your time. If you do have small children, try including them in your ritual. Have them join you in bed for those five minutes. Let them say a prayer or tell what they're grateful for, or teach them to focus on their breathing.

Personalize your ritual. You can change this ritual in whatever way feels right for you. Try setting different intentions every week or month. Examples of stress-reducing intentions are:

○ To suspend critical judgment of myself and others.
○ To be as loving a parent as I can be.
○ To see the humor in stressful moments.
○ To focus on all the positive aspects of my job.
○ To focus on all of my partner's positive qualities.
○ To become aware of all the little miracles that occur every day.

You could also try breaking the ritual into segments, doing parts of it while you're still in bed, in the shower, eating breakfast or even while you're driving to work.

Take a few moments every few hours to center yourself. You can do this by focusing on your breath and repeating an affirmation or you can repeat Thich Nhat Hanh's "wonderful moment" affirmation.

Breathing in, I calm my body.
Breathing out, I smile.
Dwelling in the present moment,
I know this is a wonderful moment!

You could also choose to focus on what you have to be grateful for in that present moment or bring your attention to your Divine connection. Don't forget to take time during the day to appreciate your surroundings, both indoors and outdoors.

Think about ending the day peacefully as well. Adapt all or parts of your morning ritual and practice it before you fall asleep each night.

This ritual, practiced throughout each day, is a great stress reducer because it allows us to focus on the positive things in our lives and reminds us to live in the present moment. The more grounded we are in the present moment the less we have to be anxious and worried about and the more opportunities we have to experience peace.

Just as important, it allows us to be in touch with our spirituality in small ways throughout each day. The benefits can be profound.

Meditation/Relaxation

Each of us has the natural ability to bring his/her body and mind to a special state which simultaneously lowers blood pressure and heart rate, decreases breathing rate, slows brain waves and reduces the speed of metabolism. This state is actually able to counteract the harmful physical effects and the uncomfortable emotional effects of stress. It also has the capacity to change the mental patterns or "worry cycles" that cause the mind to play the same anxieties or negative, health-impairing thoughts over and over again. In other words, it creates opposite effects of the stress response.

This state is most often associated with meditation. For most people the word *meditation* conjures an image of a Buddhist monk in a loin cloth, sitting in the lotus position in a barren hut in the mountains of Tibet. Meditation is also often perceived as a highly mysterious practice requiring religious devotion of some kind. As a result, many of us are intimidated or otherwise put off by the thought of meditating. However, there are a variety of forms of nonreligious meditation as well as other techniques which can elicit the same benefits as traditional meditation including autogenic training, progressive relaxation, guided imagery, hypnosis and yoga.

According to the Institute for Noetic Sciences, over 1500 studies on the effectiveness of meditation have been published since 1931. Since that time, and particularly more recently, researchers have shown that meditation is an effective strategy component in the treatment of a wide variety of physical and emotional illnesses. Meditation has been used with thousands of patients at the Mind/Body Medical Institute at New England Deaconess Hospital and Harvard Medical School, the Stress Reduction Clinic at the University of Massachusetts Medical Center and elsewhere in the treatment of physical and psychological symptoms including but not limited to the following:

- Hypertension
- Coronary heart disease
- Gastrointestinal disorders
- Sleep disorders
- Headache
- Diabetes
- Asthma
- Cancer
- AIDS/HIV
- Anxiety
- Anger
- Allergies
- Skin disorders
- Premenstrual syndrome
- Parkinson's disease
- Lupus
- Pain
- Infertility
- Hostility
- Depression

In addition to the health benefits associated with meditation, mediators experience emotional benefits. In fact, psychologist Patricia Carrington found that meditation was an effective substitute for tranquilizers. Meditators participating in her research studies have reported such emotional/psychological benefits as:

- Clearer thinking
- Less jittery
- Decreased sense of urgency
- Increased energy, productivity, efficiency
- Decrease in anxiety
- Easier to get along with
- Less irritable
- Less critical of self and others
- Less influenced by others

- Decreased feelings of pressure
- More open emotionally
- Less defensive
- Decrease in mild depression
- More self-aware
- Stronger sense of inner strength/internal validation

In a sense, we meditate all day long because we are constantly focusing our attention or awareness on something. The problem is that stressed and anxious people tend to focus their attention on negative things which they interpret as threats to their well-being. A more healthy way of focusing our attention is to use meditation to become aware of and let go of our negative thinking and to reprogram our thoughts so that threats are transformed into opportunities.

All meditation techniques have certain attributes in common. All attempt to quiet the body and mind by focusing attention or awareness on one particular object, often referred to as a centering device. A centering device can be anything you choose. More traditional centering devices include the breath, body postures (yoga), exercises (progressive muscle relaxation, autogenic training), images (imagined or real), thoughts (affirmations) and words (mantras).

In *Controlling Stress and Tension,* the authors describe the commonalities among ways to quiet the mind and the body as follows:

> . . . the one element common to all explanations is the process of trying to eliminate the surface chatter of the mind, the constant thinking, planning, remembering and fantasizing that occupies the mind every waking second and keeps the ego firmly planted in the consciousness. As the ego chatter diminishes so do the ego defenses. Anxiety is reduced, thus arousal is reduced as both the body and the mind achieve the quiet and peace natural to the ego- or self-transcendent state of consciousness.

STRATEGIES

There are five basic requirements in order to achieve the physical, psychological and emotional benefits of meditation:

1. Make meditation your express intention by setting aside the time to do it.

2. Find a quiet, comfortable place where you will not be disturbed. (Experienced meditators, however, find they can meditate almost anywhere.)

3. Assume a comfortable position in which it is possible to relax your muscles.

4. Select a centering device (a focus for your attention as a means of stopping the mental chatter). Various centering devices will be discussed below.

5. Adopt a passive attitude. This involves letting go of thoughts and feelings as they enter your awareness and gently returning to your centering device.

Given these basic elements, there are a variety of approaches, involving different centering devices, which can be used to quiet the mind and the body. Following are simple, straightforward explanations of several effective approaches. In preparation for meditation/relaxation, begin each of the following approaches by closing your eyes (unless otherwise specified), focusing on your breath and taking several deep diaphragmatic breaths, expanding your belly as you inhale and drawing it in as you exhale.

Muscle tension relaxation

This approach requires isolating the major muscle groups throughout the body and systematically tensing and relaxing them. Starting with your forehead, move through each muscle group one by one as follows:

1. Inhale.

2. Tense or squeeze the muscles of your forehead together. Hold for a count of five.

3. Exhale and relax.

4. Repeat two times.

5. Move sequentially to the cheeks, mouth and jaw, tongue, neck, shoulders, arms, hands, back, stomach, buttocks, thighs, legs, calves and finally to the feet. Alternatively, you

may begin with your feet and move through the muscle groups in the opposite direction.

Caution: Do not use this technique on parts of your body which may be weak or injured, as in the case of back problems or TMJ. Consult your physician or physical therapist to make appropriate adjustments.

Autogenic relaxation

Autogenic relaxation occurs when the mind asks the body to relax. The procedure is similar to muscle tension relaxation in that you move through each of the major areas of the body; however, you do not tense the muscles. Instead you focus your attention on a particular body part, becoming aware of the degree of tension/relaxation there and simply allowing that body part to relax more fully. For example, beginning with the feet:

Become aware of your feet, the weight of your feet pressing down on the floor, the space your feet occupy, the socks or shoes you are wearing, the skin covering your feet and all the bones and muscles and nerves inside your feet. Ask your feet to relax. Imagine breathing in through your nose and breathing out through your feet, letting your breath carry away any tension you may have had in your feet. Feel your feet relaxing more and more with each exhale. Notice how good it feels to relax your feet.

Next, move sequentially through your body parts: ankles, calves, knees, thighs, pelvis, abdomen and lower back, chest and upper back, shoulders, arms, hands, neck, scalp, forehead, eyes, cheeks, jaw, throat.

Breath meditation

The centering device in this meditation is the breathing process. Take slow deep breaths finding your own comfortable rhythm. Focus your awareness on each part of the breath as you are experiencing it—from inhale to exhale to the pauses between each inhale and exhale. Become aware of the rhythm of your breathing. If your mind wanders, simply bring it back gently to your breath.

Mantra meditation

Mantra meditation consists of the breath meditation described above, but adds the component of internally repeating a sound (*om*), a word (*one*), a phrase (*may I be peaceful*), or a prayer in rhythm with your inhaling or exhaling breath. Selecting a mantra is a matter of personal choice. Choose a word or phrase that is meaningful to you in some way and allow this to be your centering device.

Affirmation meditation

Affirmation meditation is similar to mantra meditation except that the centering device is a positive, present-tense statement which reflects a mental, emotional or physical state you want to make your own. Following are some effective stress-reducing affirmations. Choose one that is right for you.

I am relaxed.
I am calm, centered and relaxed.
Relaxation comes easy to me.
My breathing is deep and regular.
I am in control of my mind and my body.
I manage my stress effortlessly and easily.

Letting go of thoughts

The centering device in this meditation is puffy, white clouds. Allow yourself to form a picture in your mind's eye of a sky filled with puffy, white clouds. Adopting a passive attitude, watch the clouds as they move in and out of your awareness. As thoughts or feelings move into your awareness, simply observe them, without becoming attached to them, and allow them to be transformed into puffy, white clouds that gently drift out of your awareness.

Imagery/visualization

The centering device in this meditation can be any image which makes you safe and peaceful. Common images involve being at the ocean or in a meadow. As you focus on your safe, peaceful place, allow yourself to be there in your mind as fully as possible by using all of your senses to imagine what smells, sights, sounds, taste and touch sensations may be present.

Being in the present moment

The centering device in this type of meditation involves being in the present moment with whatever it is you are doing whether it is eating, walking, sitting, working at a task or simply observing something. Being in the present moment means that you are attending only to what is happening right now. It requires letting go of thoughts which involve the past or the future. It means focusing your full attention and awareness on the information coming in from all of your senses. Any activity or nonactivity can be turned into a meditation if you allow yourself to focus only on what you are doing right now. For example:

Active Present-Moment Meditation. Eating a piece of fruit in the present moment involves focusing only and completely on everything required to eat a piece of fruit, from the way your hand holds the fruit and brings it to your mouth to the way you bite into it with your teeth and how that feels, to how it tastes and feels in your mouth and when you swallow it. It also involves taking extra time to pause between each bite, to chew each mouthful 20 or 30 times, to be aware of as many sensations as possible and to let go of any thoughts that do not pertain to eating the fruit.

Nonactive Present-Moment Meditation. Bring your focus of attention to just being. Experience the rhythm of your breathing. Become aware of what you are sitting or lying on and how your body feels on it. Open your awareness to include all your senses, becoming aware of what sights, sounds, smells, tastes and textures may be present. Simply be fully immersed in the moment.

Guided meditation/relaxation tapes and books

For people who have difficulty with the approaches just described, it is possible to achieve the positive effects of meditation by following relaxation training, guided visualization and meditation programs on audiotape. There are a wide variety of tapes available which lead the listener through the meditation process. Often, beginners find these tapes helpful because they do not have to worry about whether they are doing it right. Tapes can also make the experience more pleasurable by adding music and other relaxing sounds as well as providing interesting imagery. To order my meditation/relaxation tape see page 200.

There are also many excellent book guides to meditation and relaxation which can assist you in developing the practice further. Among them are: Jon Kabat-Zinn's *Full Catastrophe Living*, Herbert Benson's *Relaxation Response* and any work by Thich Nhat Hanh.

Questions about meditation practice

Common concerns which arise from the practice of meditation/ relaxation include: "I'm not sure I'm doing it right, I was distracted, I couldn't keep my mind focused on what I was supposed to be doing, I didn't feel anything, It feels different every time, I fall asleep." The goal of meditation is not perfection, but simply to become aware of when we are distracted and to gently bring ourselves back to the meditation focus whether it be the breath, a thought, an image or any other centering device. This is what is meant by adopting a passive attitude. There is no perfect way to meditate nor perfect feeling to achieve, and the experience may well be different every time. It is the act of continually letting go of distracting thoughts and feelings and coming back to the centering device which trains us to choose our focus of concentration and achieve quiet in our minds and bodies. If you continually fall asleep during meditation it may be a sign that more sleep is needed or that a new position is needed. Meditating in a seated position is often a remedy for those who fall asleep while meditating.

• How Long Should I Practice?

In general, 20 to 30 minutes once or twice a day is a good rule of thumb. However, each person is different, and it is important that you develop a meditation practice that you can commit to and feel comfortable with. Some people find it helpful to build up the time spent meditating from a few minutes to 20 or 30 minutes per day. Others find it helpful to begin with a guided relaxation tape with someone directing the meditation. In times of extreme anxiety, it is helpful to meditate several times a day.

• Common Objections

Common objections to making the practice of meditation/relaxation a part of one's lifestyle include: "I don't have time, I'm too stressed to meditate, It won't work for me, It's too difficult, I'd rather just take a pill." The bottom line is that meditation is one of the most effective, non-pharmaceutical strategies for managing stress. Decreased stress response can be achieved in a matter of days. Moreover, meditation does not cost anything, nor does it require elaborate preparation; the meditator is in complete control. Meditation requires a concentrated and committed effort, but the benefits far outweigh the perceived inconveniences.

• Side Effects

Trauma. In rare cases people who have experienced severe trauma may have certain negative reactions to meditation such as flashbacks. Although this is a rare occurrence, therapists should take this into consideration before recommending a client practice meditation when alone. I have found that with clients who may be experiencing post-traumatic stress syndrome and/or severe anxiety, it is important to begin the practice of relaxation training/meditation during a client session in order to determine the client's likely reaction. Then I suggest using guided relaxation training/meditation tapes as a first step to practice at home.

Clients are likely to focus more fully on the speaker's directions, which may inhibit intrusive thoughts and/or images. It is also important to give the client strategies for grounding and regaining a feeling of safety if the client experiences a negative reaction. The therapist needs to carefully and gently prepare the trauma client for the low risk of a negative reaction to meditation while avoiding predisposing the client to such a reaction via suggestion.

Medications. On a positive note, researchers have found that the need for medications taken for such conditions as asthma, diabetes and high blood pressure may be reduced with regular meditation practice. For this reason it is critical that clients on medication for these conditions continue to be monitored by their physicians.

Discomfort. New meditators may experience minimal side effects such as jumping or twitching muscles, a slight tingling sensation or other symptoms typical of the body beginning to relax. Such side effects generally occur within the first 10 minutes of meditation and are likely to disappear within several days of practice.

Some clients may feel uncomfortable when they allow themselves to relax because it is such an unfamiliar experience for them. Some clients have even said that relaxation/meditation makes them tense. Unless there are issues of trauma, this is a good sign that they need to stay with the practice in order to train themselves to experience and become comfortable with the pleasurable benefits of relaxation/meditation. Although it is very rare, if a person does become overly anxious, depressed or otherwise distressed as a direct result of meditating, there are other relaxation methods which can be substituted, such as video tapes featuring music/scenery or using healing images or affirmations.

Mind/Body Checks

Once you have become comfortable with healing breath work and meditation you will be able to use Mind/Body Checks throughout the day as a means of preventing stress build-up or as a means of tuning in to your stress level and turning it down. Mind/Body Checks involve taking a brief break from what you are doing to tune in to the state of your mind and your body in the following way:

STRATEGY

Sitting quietly in a relaxed position and leaving legs and arms uncrossed, take a few deep healing breaths. As you focus on your breathing, take a moment to scan your body, beginning with your feet and moving up through the rest of your body, becoming aware of any areas of tension. If you become aware of an area of tension, gently allow yourself to relax that area and direct your breath there as if you could exhale your breath into it. Continue until you have scanned through your whole body. As you become more aware of where you hold your tension, you may be able to focus right in on those areas without scanning your whole body. For example, many people hold tension in their neck and shoulders.

Once you have scanned your body, take a moment to become aware of what is happening in your mind. Adopt a passive attitude and make note of your thoughts and feelings. Having made note of them, allow the mental chatter to quiet down as you focus on your breathing. This is a good time to repeat any special stress-reducing affirmations you may have developed for yourself.

Mind/Body Checks can be as brief as the time it takes to take three healing breaths or as long as three minutes. Three minutes represents a small fraction of the 1,440 minutes in a day. Spend as much or as little time as you want to or need to. Most importantly, by allowing yourself the opportunity to tune in to the state of your mind/body you can prevent stress build-up and lower the negative effects of stress before they become a problem. Each time you allow yourself to reset your stress level throughout the day you are giving yourself an opportunity to interrupt the stress response and allowing endorphins to flow which give you a sense of well-being. With proper use of Mind/Body Checks you are also giving yourself a chance to work and/or play more efficiently and productively.

Identifying Negative Self-Talk

Do you find yourself saying things to yourself like: "What a jerk I am; how stupid can I be; it's all my fault; I'm worthless; everyone notices how imperfect I am; everyone sees the stupid things I do; I should always do the right thing; I either do it perfectly or I'm a failure; I am incapable of changing; I'm trapped; something bad always happens to ruin my happiness; nothing ever goes right for me; I always screw things up; I don't deserve to be happy; the bad things that happen to me are a punishment for not being good enough; nothing ever goes right for me"?

Many people who experience a great deal of stress are constantly beating themselves up with these kinds of negative thoughts. In fact, if we could really be aware of the cruel way we talk to ourselves we would be horrified by the level of emotional abuse we heap upon ourselves.

Remember my definition of stress: We experience stress when we tell ourselves something negative about ourselves and our ability to cope with circumstances, events, conditions or people we encounter in our daily lives. So when we talk to ourselves this way we become our own greatest stressor. In other words, we are the greatest source of our own stress.

We all engage in internal self-talk; we all talk to ourselves. Some of our internal self-talk is positive, some neutral and some of it is negative. Those of us who experience stress and anxiety are often likely to engage in negative self-talk a great deal. That is, we criticize ourselves for having or not having done something, said something, or even thought something. This type of self-talk is often referred to as "the inner critic." The inner critic's job is to blame us, remind us of our failures, attack us with words like stupid, lazy, weak, inadequate. The inner critic reminds us that we have to be perfect, tells us what we should and should not do and generally tries to block any positive messages we might give ourselves. When we allow ourselves to be occupied with negative and critical thoughts about ourselves we are, in effect, beating ourselves up. This lowers our self-esteem which in turn lowers our resistance to stress.

In stress management terminology, we condemn ourselves for not being appropriate or acting appropriately in response to a potential stressor. And this is exactly the condition that triggers the experience of stress—telling ourselves something negative about our ability to cope with a potential stressor.

STRATEGIES

Negative self-talk is not only the most powerful trigger of stress and anxiety, it extends, maintains and perpetuates stress. The first step in dealing with this powerful trigger is to become aware of when and how we engage in negative self-talk.

o For one day, keep a written log of each time you engage in negative self-talk or beat yourself up. Pay attention to how often it occurs, under what circumstances, and what you are telling yourself about yourself. Continue keeping this log until you can clearly identify when and how you put yourself down.

o Whenever you are feeling stressed or anxious take a time-out: stop, take a few healing breaths and become aware of what you are telling yourself about the situation, about yourself and about your ability to cope with the circumstances you find yourself in. Remember, when you are stressed or anxious your first instinct may be to tell yourself something negative about yourself.

Recognizing Distorted Thinking

Once you have trained yourself to become aware of negative thoughts it is important to examine how accurate these negative thoughts are. We know from cognitive theory that thoughts precede feelings and that negative thoughts will give rise to negative feelings.

Cognitive researchers tell us that 99 percent of all negative thoughts which cause emotional turmoil contain gross distortions. These distortions color our perception of potential stressors, making us less objective about our ability to cope and making it more likely that we will experience stress. These distortions not only represent dysfunctional thinking, they also represent the strategies that our critic uses to beat us up emotionally.

Psychologist Aaron Beck originally developed a set of categories to describe this type of dysfunctional thinking for the professional literature. Later, Dr. David Burns, in his excellent book, *The Feeling Good Handbook*, created a layman's version of cognitive distortions or "twisted thinking" as he refers to it. In my work, I generally focus on five types of distorted thinking. See if you can recognize some of the ways in which you might engage in it.

1. **Black or White Thinking.** Also referred to as *dichotomous thinking, polarized thinking, or all-or-nothing thinking*. This occurs when we look at things in terms of absolutes or extremes. It occurs when we don't consider all our possible options, when we refuse to see the merits of a situation, when we don't consider the "gray area," or when we consider anything less than perfection a failure. For example: "If the weather isn't perfect on my vacation, I will have a lousy time." "If the Patriots don't win the Superbowl, the whole season is a total loss." "If I don't pass the bar exam on the first try, I will be a failure." "My life will be ruined if I don't get this job . . . get married . . . have children . . . buy this house."

2. **Assumptions.** Also referred to as *arbitrary inference, mind-reading* and *jumping to conclusions*. This means that we draw conclusions without having all the necessary information, and in many cases, not having any reasonable or reliable information. For example, "Anything that can go wrong will go wrong." "Because my husband didn't run to greet me when I came home, he must be mad at me." "The school bus is late; there must have been an accident." "My friend didn't call this week; she doesn't want to talk to me." In assump-

tions of blame we can either take on the responsibility for things that are not our fault or we blame other people instead of accepting responsibility for our own actions. For example, "It's my fault the clothes on the clothesline got wet when it rained." "It's my fault that my husband knocked over the vase because I put it there." "It's my fault the baby woke up when I walked into the room." "I'm to blame for my son flunking math; I was never any good at it." "If my husband had parked the car correctly, I wouldn't have run over the rose bush." "If I didn't have children, I would have been able to pursue my career as a singer . . . I would have gotten my college degree . . . I wouldn't have gained this weight." "It's my boss's fault that I didn't get that promotion—he didn't try hard enough." "If he didn't make me angry, I wouldn't have been so mean."

The bottom line here is that all assumptions are dangerous. You know the old saying which plays on the spelling of the word assume: "Assuming makes an ass out of you and me." I have seen a great deal of pain, heartache, incredibly bad judgment and ruined relationships result from making assumptions. Get the facts. Ask questions. When in doubt, do what you have to do to get the right information before you waste precious energy on making an assumption.

3. **Excessive Self-Criticism.** Also referred to as *labeling, emotional reasoning* and *"shoulding" on yourself.* This is another dangerous way of beating ourselves up—we make negative value judgments about ourselves and criticize ourselves relentlessly for every real or imagined imperfection or mistake. For example: "I'm worthless . . . lazy . . . stupid . . . foolish . . . a jerk . . . a loser." "I should be the perfect wife . . . mother . . . lover . . . worker all the time." "I'm selfish to want to take time for myself . . . spend money for my health/personal growth." "I don't deserve to be happy . . . have things go right . . . be in a good relationship." "There's something wrong with me . . . I'm not like anyone else . . . I'm different."

4. **Negative Expectations.** Also referred to as *using a mental filter, tunnel vision, discounting the positives, magnification (of*

the negative). When we allow ourselves to have negative expectations we exclude anything positive that has occurred or might occur. We look in our environment and see only those things that prove our negative view. We tend to blow things out of proportion because we don't take the positive aspects of the situation into consideration. In other words, there is no balance to our thinking and therefore less chance of seeing things objectively or finding reasons to be hopeful. For example: "If I play on the team (or bet on the team) they'll lose." You tell yourself that you'll hate going to New York City because all you see is litter and homeless people, even though you love and enjoy the wide variety of food and cultural experiences. Perhaps a friend once snapped at you when he was having a bad day and even though he's never done it again, you're forever on guard.

5. **Overgeneralizing.** When we overgeneralize we tend to take one experience we've had and tell ourselves that every situation like that or even close to that experience will have the same negative outcome. For example: "I hated playing field hockey in high school so I won't enjoy participating in any group sports." "I tried one dance lesson and couldn't catch on so I will never be able to learn to dance." After each break-up of a relationship you tell yourself, "I will never find the right partner." "I get nervous talking in front of people, I will never be able to give a speech or make a presentation." "Because I once got fired, I will never succeed in my career."

Eliminating Negative Self-Talk and Distorted Thinking

Once we recognize our negative self-talk we need to fire our inner critic. Much of the way we think has been programmed into us as children by the significant people in our lives. Just as thoughts can be programmed, they can also be reprogrammed. In fact, we can choose the way we think. If we can choose the way we think, we can also choose the way we feel and behave.

STRATEGY

In order to begin reprogramming distorted or stressful thinking we first must become aware of the circumstances in which the thought and related feelings occur. By understanding ways in which we might be distorting our thinking we can begin to evaluate our thoughts more objectively and begin to construct a more rational, balanced and positive thought replacement. Cognitive therapists use several variations of the following technique. Examine your negative thoughts or messages from your inner critic and keep a record of them in the following way:

1. Recognize when you are having a negative thought or when your critic is talking.
2. Make note of the situation you are in when these thoughts occur.
3. Identify the negative thought.
4. Identify the subsequent feeling.
5. Identify the ways in which that thought might be distorted.
6. Based on those distortions, reframe your perception to be more objective and positive.

EXAMPLES:

I. Situation: Boss asks to see me.
Negative thought: "Oh no, he's mad at me."
Feeling: Fear, Anxiety.
Distortion(s): Engaging in negative expectations by dwelling on unfavorable reasons why the boss might want to see me or forgetting that the boss also asks to see me for good reasons. Making assumptions by attempting to read the boss's mind or predict the future.
Objective/positive thought: "I see that I am distorting my thinking in a number of ways. There is no reason for me to believe that the boss is mad at me so I will assume that everything is fine until he tells me otherwise."

II. Situation: My child caught a cold.
Negative thought: "What an idiot I am . . . It's my fault . . . I should never have let her play outside without a hat."

Feeling: Anger (at self).
Distortion(s): Using shoulds to criticize myself. Labeling myself by identifying myself as an idiot. Using emotional reasoning. Blaming myself for something I wasn't entirely responsible for.
Objective/positive thought: "I see that I am distorting my thinking in a number of ways. It's not my fault she caught a cold. Germs create cold symptoms not cold weather. She could have picked up the cold anywhere. I may have made a mistake by not dressing her warmly enough, but I do not have to be perfect. Now I want to focus on getting her well again with lots of love, rest and hot chicken soup!"

Evaluating and Eliminating the "Shoulds"

Before moving to the next step in firing the critic it is important to scrutinize a particularly treacherous cognitive distortion, the "shoulds," statements which criticize ourselves and others with such absolutes as *must, always, never* or *perfect*. Psychoanalyst Karen Horney tells us that the critic rules on all that we should be able to do, to be, to feel, to know, and sets limits on how and what we should or should not be. Exactly like a political dictator, the critic operates with a supreme disregard for one's feelings or capabilities.

For the purpose of this discussion, the "shoulds" refers to all terminology that infers absolute adherence to any belief, rule or value. As stated earlier, many of our strongest beliefs are programmed into us in childhood. These beliefs and rules are formed in response to needs which may have nothing to do with truth or reality. They are generated by parental, cultural, religious and peer expectations and by our needs to feel loved and approved of, to belong and to feel safe and good about ourselves. In our desire for love and safety we adopted our parents' beliefs. And if we did not live up to those values and were criticized as lazy, stupid, selfish and so on, we often accepted those judgments as well. So the critic represents that part of us which internalized the rules of others and their criticisms for not living up to those rules.

Shoulds imply an inflexibility and rigidity that do not apply to this imperfect world and to the imperfect beings that we are. Listed below are some of the more stressful shoulds:

o I should always be perfect and do everything perfectly.
o I should be the best spouse, parent, friend, worker.
o I should never make mistakes.
o I should know and anticipate everything.
o I should never feel hurt, angry or sad.
o I should always be in control.
o I should like/love everyone.
o Everyone should like/love me.
o I should never have any problems.
o I should always put the needs of others before mine; other-
       wise I am being selfish.
o I should always be honest, generous and unselfish.

When we adopt the "shoulds" of others and never examine them in terms of our own needs, desires and capabilities we are setting ourselves up for the experience of stress and anxiety. These "shoulds" leave no room for compromise or exception. As a result, "shoulds" often give rise to a feeling of being trapped, which represents a threat, and threatening thoughts trigger the stress response. Because "shoulds" are inflexible and rigid, they also represent the threat of failure and guilt and these threats offer the perfect opportunity for the critic to go to work.

When we are unable to live up to these "shoulds" and we allow the critic to beat us up for not doing so, we are, in effect, telling ourselves that we are unable to cope with the situation which provoked our "shoulds." As a result, the should-critic sequence automatically triggers the stress response.

For example, here are some "shoulds" which might be programmed into us by our parents. As such, they fall into the category of putting others' needs before our own.

o "I should visit my parents every Sunday."
o "I should go into the family business."
o "I should become a doctor (lawyer, policeman, professor, etc.)."

"I should visit my parents every Sunday" does not allow for the flexibility of making other plans for the day or for accepting invitations or commitments which might fall on a Sunday. In today's hectic world, with two-career families and various activities for children it is unrealistic to believe that this "should" can be carried out without a large degree of internal conflict and struggle. If we put our parents' needs/wants first we lose out on other important experiences and perhaps feel angry about that. If we decide to do something other than visit our parents but remain emotionally tied into the "should" by feeling guilty, the critic will assault us with messages like: "What's the matter with you, your selfishness is hurting your parents."

"I should go into the family business" and "I should become a doctor or whatever my parents want me to do" means that I must ignore my own interests and desires in order to live out the desires of others. This "should" requires that I disregard my own unique talents and abilities and spend my working life doing something that may not suit me or satisfy me. If I really want to be an artist but decide to follow my parents' wishes and become a doctor I may end up feeling unfulfilled and trapped in a career I don't enjoy. If I choose to pursue a career as an artist, the critic may haunt me with messages like: "Being an artist is foolish and frivolous; you'll never really be successful or make enough money."

STRATEGY

In a healthy value system there are no "shoulds," there are only choices. The first task in moving from "shoulds" to choices is to look for and be aware of your "shoulds" as you say them to yourself or to someone else. Whenever you hear yourself using the word *should* or any other word such as *must, ought to, never, always, perfect* or *have to,* stop yourself and do the following:

1. Ask yourself whether you have truly examined this belief for yourself in terms of your own unique needs, desires and lifestyle or whether this value was programmed into you. If you have never taken the time to evaluate this belief, take the time to do so.

2. Ask yourself whether this particular "should" is realistic and flexible enough to be appropriate to any and all circumstances.

3. Replace the phrase, "I should (must, ought to, etc.)" with "I choose to" and see how that changes how you feel about what you are saying. Remember, thoughts lead to feelings. Thoughts which include words like *should* imply guilt, obligation and/or being trapped. Thoughts which include words like *choose* imply willingness, want and desire. In stress management terms, a sense of choice tends to negate the perception of being unable to cope, thereby preventing the stress repsonse from being triggered. An added benefit here is that we also have the opportunity to feel better about our decision because we are looking at it from the perspective of what we really want.

4. Work to eliminate *should* words from your language.

Consider the example, "I should always be perfect." You are learning a new skill like sign language, horseback riding or cooking. As you are practicing, you hear yourself telling yourself some variation of the should statement—"I should get it right the first time." Stop and ask yourself: "Is this really my belief or is it part of my programming which comes to me automatically when I am attempting to learn something new? Is this belief realistic and flexible?" Your answer might be: "No, that is what my mother used to expect of me. I realize that this is a new skill for me and I might make some mistakes. It isn't realistic for me to expect that I will get it right the first time. It takes time to acquire new skills." Then replace "should" with "I choose to get it right the first time." You might find, based on your examination of this should, that choosing to get it right the first time does not feel right to you so you might replace your automatic "should" phrase with "I choose to allow myself to make mistakes as I learn this new skill."

Look again at the example, "I should visit my parents every Sunday." The strategy for eliminating "shoulds" might reveal to you that this belief is really a value passed down to you from your parents. Perhaps they view the Sunday ritual as an expression of love. But life was different when they grew up. People lived and worked close to home. There may not have been as many time pressures and obligations to be involved in activities outside of the family. So this belief might not fit you and your lifestyle. Perhaps there are other ways you can express your love. So when you say to yourself, "I choose to visit my parents every Sunday," that may not feel comfortable. A more realistic belief and choice for you might be: "I choose to visit my parents on Sundays when I don't have another commitment that is important to me."

Using Affirmations

Negative self-talk and "shoulds" affect the way we perceive and experience ourselves, other people and what happens to us. Negative thinking from our childhood programming tends to repeat itself over and over like an endless tape loop until it becomes so automatic we are not even aware of it. The problem is that each time we have a negative thought our brains send a message to our bodies that there is a potential threat occurring and the body goes on alert via the stress response. Since every thought we think gets transmitted to every cell in our bodies within 1/100th of a second, an automatic thought will lead to an almost instantaneous reaction in the body.

In order to combat the stress created by negative thinking we must reprogram ourselves with positive thoughts so the brain is not sending danger signals to the body needlessly. Some of the components for re-programming include:

o Learning to have compassion for ourselves.
o Learning to talk to ourselves in a relaxing and comforting manner.
o Learning to talk ourselves out of being anxious or fearful in situations where we might be distorting our thinking.
o Learning to sincerely acknowledge and honor our own successes.

○ Learning to use positive instead of negative self-talk when we feel we have been unsuccessful at something or made a mistake.

○ Learning to stop negative self-talk and replace it with positive self-talk.

Our thoughts often become self-fulfilling prophecies so, rather than engaging in negative thinking and creating stress for ourselves, it is important to think more objectively, more positively. An added benefit of positive thinking is that we begin to perceive and experience ourselves, other people and what happens to us more favorably and affirmatively. As we have seen from the research on hope and optimism, our thoughts are very powerful. Examples of the power of positive thinking include people with spinal cord injuries who experience more improved functioning and cancer patients who live longer and with a better quality of life.

One very effective way to program ourselves to think more positively is to use affirmations. Affirmations are also a means of programming ourselves to create what we want for ourselves. They reinforce our beliefs and/or desires about what we can do and how we want to be. Louise Hay describes an affirmation as a present-tense statement which reflects a mental, emotional or physical state you would like to be experiencing. In their *Wellness Workbook*, John Travis and Regina Ryan describe an affirmation as "a verbal description of a desired condition." Steven Covey, author of *Seven Habits of Highly Effective People*, reports that there are five basic ingredients in a good affirmation. The affirmation has to be personal, positive, in the present tense, visual and emotional. The more we choose to think positively, the more we counteract and dispel our negative thinking.

STRATEGY

1. When you find yourself experiencing stress or anxiety, stop and ask yourself how you would like to feel or what you would like to be experiencing.

2. Create a statement that reflects how you would like to feel or what you would like to experience.

3. Make the statement personal by using "I" statements and by making the statement meaningful to you, both in the words you choose and the intention and commitment you feel about what it is you want.

4. Put the statement in the present tense.

5. Make sure the statement is positive and that it contains no negative words like *not, never*.

6. Form a visual image of yourself achieving or attaining what it is you desire.

7. Repeat your affirmation as often during the day as possible. Remind yourself to repeat your affirmation when you wake up in the morning, while you are taking a shower, eating a meal, driving in your car, meditating, breathing and before going to sleep at night. Repetition is important to combat the many times you may have thought negatively about the same situation.

For example, an affirmation might be helpful to you when trying to complete a project on a deadline. Rather than focusing on all the reasons why it might not be possible to complete the project and letting that negative thinking trigger and maintain the stress response, create an affirmation to focus on. An appropriate affirmation might be: "I am completing my project easily and effortlessly." The statement is personal, it should 'feel' good, and it is in the present tense. It is also positive. Developing the affirmation alone is not enough; it is critical to visualize the affirmation coming true and to say the affirmation often during the day.

Following are good examples of stress-reducing affirmations you can use during meditation and/or at various stress points in your day. A good stress management technique is to stop for a moment, concentrate on your breathing and repeat some of these affirmations to yourself:

o I am calm and relaxed.
o I feel peaceful and centered.
o My breathing is deep and regular.

○ I am breathing in calming energy and exhaling tension.
○ My mind, my emotions and my body are at peace.
○ I choose to create balance and harmony in my life.
○ I am in control of my mind, my emotions and my body.
○ I manage my stress effectively.
○ I choose to create a lifestyle for myself which nurtures and supports my well-being.
○ I have control over how I react to stressful situations in my life.
○ My body and mind work in harmony to keep me healthy and happy.
○ I am worthy and deserving of happiness.
○ I am creating everything I need for my emotional, physical and spiritual well-being.
○ I am moving through my day easily and effortlessly.

Make up your own affirmations. Simply make up a *positive, present-tense* statement which reflects a mental, emotional or physical state you would like to be experiencing. Make sure it has meaning and emotion, visualize it, and practice it often each day until you have achieved it. You may want to begin your affirmations with:

○ I am . . .
○ I am in control . . .
○ I am creating . . .
○ I can . . .
○ I deserve to . . .
○ I choose to . . .

Affirmations represent a particularly powerful strategy for re-programming negative thoughts. Use affirmations to interrupt and replace negative self-talk. Affirmations are also very effective when combined with Eliminating Negative Self-talk and Distorted Thinking and Evaluating and Eliminating the "Shoulds." Once you have identified a stressful distortion or "should," create an affirmation that is specifically designed to combat that negative self-talk you identified.

Identifying Your Needs

People who experience high degrees of stress and anxiety are either unaware of their needs or are aware of their needs but not working to get them met. Once we are able to identify our needs and master the ability to get those needs met it is possible to experience a significant reduction in stress and anxiety symptoms.

Charles Whitfield has expanded on the basic needs work of others like Abraham Maslow and compiled a hierarchy of human needs, which follows:

WHITFIELD'S HIERARCHY OF HUMAN NEEDS

1. Survival
2. Safety
3. Touching, skin contact
4. Attention
5. Mirroring and echoing
6. Guidance
7. Listening
8. Being real
9. Participating and connecting
10. Acceptance from yourself and others
    - Others are aware of, take seriously and admire the real you
    - Freedom to be the real you
    - Tolerance of your feelings
    - Validation
    - Respect
    - Belonging and love
11. Opportunity to grieve losses and to grow
12. Support
13. Loyalty and trust
14. Accomplishment
    - Mastery, power, control
    - Creativity

- ○ Having a sense of completion
- ○ Making a contribution
15. Altering one's state of consciousness, transcending the ordinary (feeling a part of the universe)
16. Sexuality
17. Enjoyment or fun
18. Freedom
19. Nurturing
20. Unconditional love (including connection with a Higher Power)

Needs can also be expressed in terms of human rights. Several versions of a cognitive/emotional Bill of Rights have been developed to illustrate individual human rights. This version is by Ruth Sharon, M.S., L.P.C. of Englewood, Colorado.

ASSERTIVE BILL OF RIGHTS

I have the right to:

- ○ be responsible for my own life.
- ○ support others being responsible for themselves.
- ○ create conscious interdependence in my life (we're all here together).
- ○ accept and respect myself and others.
- ○ feel happy, satisfied, and to allow inner peace.
- ○ take good care of my whole being: my body, my mind and my spirit.
- ○ be imperfect, and to forgive myself and others for our mistakes.
- ○ be aware of and fulfill my own needs (and to support others doing so also).
- ○ have dreams, goals and ideals—and to bring them into reality.
- ○ have and express all my emotions, without indulgence.
- ○ tell others how I want to be treated.
- ○ allow people to help me even if I'm feeling guilty, unworthy or dependent.

○ set my own priorities for the use of time, money, space and energy.
○ get what I pay for.
○ get paid what I deserve.
○ have healthy, life-enhancing relationships.
○ change, emerge, expand in new directions.
○ free myself from guilt and worry, and trust the goodness of myself.
○ work together with others to resolve conflict and create a world beyond war.

STRATEGY

Go through the *Hierarchy of Human Needs* and the *Assertive Bill of Rights,* and ask yourself two questions for each item:

1. Is this basic human need/right operating in my life?
2. Is it operating in my life to the extent that I want/need it to?

In answering these two questions you are allowing yourself to become more aware of what your needs are and whether your needs are being met. If you have needs that are not being met they may be triggering stress or anxiety symptoms.

Getting Your Needs Met

The *Hierarchy of Human Needs* and the *Assertive Bill of Rights* may also lead you to think of other important needs/wants that are not being met in your life. Once you have identified what is lacking in your life, you have the opportunity and the power to begin to seek out options for fulfilling those needs. Taking action to get our needs met not only reduces the perception of being trapped but gives us a healthy sense of control in our lives. Some basic rules for fulfilling your needs/wants include:

○ Prioritize needs/wants in order of importance. You may also want to prioritize items on your list in terms of ease of achievement. Start with the needs/wants on your list which are easiest to achieve so you can build confidence in your ability to fulfill your own needs/wants.

o Take each need on your list and make it as specific as possible. Ask yourself: what is it exactly that you need, whom do you need it from, how do you need it, and when do you need it. For example:

> *What do you need?* I need 20 minutes a day of uninterrupted time by myself so I can meditate.

> *Whom do you need it from?* I need the time from my children and my spouse.

> *How do you need it?* I need my spouse and my children not to interrupt me for any reason except an emergency of health and/or safety. (Make sure you define emergency.)

> *When do you need it?* I need this time when I come home from work.

o Make arrangements to speak with those who might be involved with getting your needs met: spouse, children, co-workers, boss, parents, friends, service person.

o Communciate your need clearly, concisely and specifically. Do not accuse or be defensive. Do not apologize. You have the right to ask for what you want.

Self-Reflection

Developing the ability to reflect on what we are thinking and feeling is another way of recognizing what our needs are in the moment and then allowing that emotional energy to provide the impetus to take action to get those needs met. Remember, when we feel stressed, angry, anxious, fearful, depressed or any combination of these feelings, we are telling ourselves something negative about our ability to cope with the situation at hand. In other words, we are telling ourselves that we are being threatened in some way. Very often we stay stuck focusing on our negative thoughts and emotions about the person or situation that appears to be causing our stress. Then we find ourselves rehashing, analyzing, judging or feeling like a victim. This diminishes our healthy sense of control and personal power.

The reason self-reflection is so important is that it allows us to move beyond our negative thoughts and feelings. We need to remember two things: 1) 99 percent of our negative thinking is self-destructive; and 2) Feelings are very powerful tools that we can use to determine whether or not our needs are being met. Real personal power and healthy control lie in reflecting on our thoughts, feelings and needs, and then doing something constructive to resolve them in a positive way.

STRATEGY

Use the following strategy when you are experiencing stress or anxiety in order to develop a deeper awareness of your thoughts and emotions and to use those emotions to get your needs met. You may also want to use this strategy when you experience happiness. It is just as important to know when you feel happy so you know your needs are getting met and you can make sure they continue to get met.

As you become aware of feeling stressed or anxious, take a deep breath and then ask yourself:

o   What am I telling myself about myself and my ability to cope with the person, event, condition or situation I am experiencing? What is the threat to me?
o   Which one of the four basic emotions am I feeling (mad, sad, glad, afraid)?
o   What physical sensations am I experiencing in my body? Use the Mind/Body Check to become aware of areas of tension in your body, your heart and breathing rhythms and any other somatic responses.
o   Am I distorting my thinking in a way which creates stress or anxiety needlessly? If the answer is no, go on to the next question. If the answer is yes, allow yourself to develop a more objective thought or affirmation in response to the situation you're experiencing. Next, watch as your feelings change in response to your more objective/positive thought.
o   What do I have control over, what don't I have control over?

○ Am I being as compassionate and loving toward myself as I could be? What can I tell myself that is more objective, compassionate or self-loving?

○ What need is not being met or what limit/boundary is not being honored?

○ How important is this need/limit/boundary to me in the present moment? Will I still care about this issue several hours from now, a day from now, a month from now, a year from now, five years from now?

○ Based on the answer to the previous question, what are my choices and what steps am I willing to take to address this need/limit/boundary?

For example, one experience of stress might arise when you do not make quiet time for yourself. You might tell yourself that you never have enough time to just relax. The feeling that arises from this thought might be anger. You might be aware of physical sensations such as tension in your forehead and neck, shallow breathing and rapid heartbeat. You might also be able to identify some distortions in your thinking. For example, you may find you are overgeneralizing or blowing things out of proportion and come to realize that you generally do have time for yourself but you do not allow yourself to take it or use it to relax. You may find a "should," such as "I should not take time for myself," is also part of your distorted thinking. A more objective thought might be, "I do have time for myself but I am not using it to relax." A useful affirmation might be, "It is healthy for me to take time for myself, and I choose to take time for myself to relax." As you think more positively, you are likely to feel better and to take steps to act on your affirmation.

The same situation might give rise to a slightly different thought, "There are too many priorities in my daily schedule and these priorities prevent me from taking time for myself to relax," but you may not find any distortions in your thinking. You may already be aware that taking time for yourself to relax is a basic human need or you may refer to the *Hierarchy of Human Needs* and *Assertive Bill of Rights* to validate this need. As you find that it is important to you to have time each day to relax and that this is a continuing need, you now have the opportunity to consider what options you have for making time each day to relax. You might ask others to help you to fulfill some of your priority activities or you might reconsider your priorities and decide that some can be eliminated or rearranged to allow you more time. Then, you need to plan how you will get this need met and start putting your plan into action.

The more you are able to bring the focus back to yourself, determining what the threat is to you, what you are feeling and what you need as a result, the more likely you will be able to take care of yourself in a healthy way. In contrast, the more you stay focused on the other person or situation and continue to spend time judging, rehashing or feeling like a victim, the less energy you will have to take care of yourself and do something constructive to get your needs met.

Coping with Worry

Worry means feeling uneasy or concerned about something; being troubled about a problem. It is a secondary emotion arising from fear which results in a cycle of continuous thoughts about a particular concern or problem. The more we indulge in worry, the more likely it is that we will become stuck in an unproductive, unhealthy cycle of anxiety. The sooner we become aware of the experience of worry, the sooner we can use it to get our needs met. "Healthy" worrying allows us to become aware of what is bothering us so we can begin the process of problem solving and positive action. We can make worrying work for us by learning what unhealthy worry is, how to engage in healthy worry and how to take action to solve problems.

Unhealthy worry starts with negative self-talk and distorted thinking. Often, we repeat such programming as, "I know I can't do it, I have to be perfect, I have to please everyone" over and over until we find ourselves unable to see options, think problems through to a solution or take action. We also engage in unhealthy worry when we think about things we have little or no control over—such as whether other people will keep their word, whether our adult children will succeed in life, or whether there will be a snowstorm.

Sometimes we worry about things we do have control over but fail to take responsibility for them, such as worrying about having a heart attack when we continue to smoke, drink too much, eat high-fat foods and/or fail to exercise. At other times we worry unnecessarily as a result of past experiences or habits. However, these worries may not have any basis in reality today. Just because you were not successful at sports or home economics in high school does not mean you cannot develop sports or domestic skills as an adult. Use the following strategy the next time you find yourself worrying.

STRATEGY

○ Listen to and evaluate your self-talk. Identify those issues you continue to talk to yourself about over and over again.
○ Use the Eliminating Negative Self-Talk and Distorted Thinking Strategy (page 116) to determine how valid your worries are.
○ Label your worries according to 1) what you have control over; and 2) what you do not have control over.
○ If you do not have control over what you are worrying about then let it go. If you find it hard to let go, create an appropriate affirmation and use it as a thought replacement.
○ If you do have control over what you are worrying about: 1) identify your choices and options; 2) create a step-by-step plan to take responsibility for what you have control over; and, 3) take action—implement your plan.
○ Once you have decided to take action, do the best that you can, remind yourself you are doing the best you can, accept the result and let it go.

Many of us worry about financial concerns such as whether we will have enough money to pay our bills and put our children through college. You may evaluate these types of worries using the strategy for recognizing distorted thinking and to determine whether your worries are valid. Since, for the most part, financial concerns are something we have control over, there are some options and choices to consider in order to take positive action. These include investing in various types of insurance policies, college funds, retirement funds, savings programs; getting a part-time job; getting a better-paying job; and developing and implementing a budget. Once you have brainstormed and considered all your options you might develop a plan that includes all or a combination of the options you have identified. As part of your action plan you might also consider what preliminary steps you might need to take before implementing one of your plans, such as getting more education in order to find a better job.

As mentioned earlier, some worries include components we have control over and components we do not have control over. For example, you may be worried about a friend or loved one who is dying from a terminal illness. On one hand, we have no control over another person dying and perhaps no control over the loss we will feel when that person dies. On the other hand, we do have control over such things as choosing when and how we might spend time with that person, what we can express to that person about how we feel and preparing ourselves emotionally for the grief process.

Dealing with Guilt

Guilt can also be healthy or unhealthy. Healthy guilt can be used to prevent us from harming ourselves, others and our environment. The anticipation of guilt helps us to adhere to a moral code, whether we choose to follow our own moral code or that set down by religion or society. Moral codes often include behavioral guidelines about killing, stealing or lying, helping to maintain order and make sense of our world. Healthy guilt motivates us to make amends for our mistakes or wrongdoings.

Guilt becomes unhealthy when we allow ourselves to dwell on our mistakes and beat ourselves up for them. Just as unhealthy worry arises from negative self-talk and distorted thinking, so, too, does guilt. Some of the guilt we experience is the result of blaming ourselves for things that are not our fault. Often children will blame themselves for problems in the family, even when they are not responsible for the problem. For example, children from alcoholic and abusive homes often tell themselves, "Mommy wouldn't drink so much if I were a better child," or "Daddy wouldn't hit me if I didn't deserve it."

We also experience guilt when we continue to blame ourselves for past or current thoughts and behaviors. We might feel guilty for not spending much time with our children or our parents, for not finishing college, for harboring resentment toward someone. Underlying our unhealthy guilt are such negative messages as, "I am a bad person if I make a mistake," and "I should be punished." More often than not, these messages involve some form of thought distortion. The more we listen to these messages, the worse we feel and the less likely we are to take any productive action to eliminate our guilt.

STRATEGY

o Identify all the things that make you feel guilty including actions you may have taken or feelings you may have about such things as relationships, food, sex, money, work, responsibilities, religion.

o Use the Eliminating Negative Self-Talk and Distorted Thinking Strategy (see pages 116-18) to determine whether your guilty thoughts and feelings are realistic and objective.

o If you still feel guilty, choose to take productive action. If you feel that you have hurt or mistreated someone, find a way to apologize to them. If there is some way to make amends for your mistake, like paying to have something repaired, do so. This is an extremely effective means of helping you to let go and move on.

o Learning from your mistakes or wrongdoings is also a way of taking productive action. Allow yourself time to honestly evaluate (without self-criticism) what you may have done, how the situation may have occurred and how you can prevent it from happening again. Develop a strategy for changing the thoughts and feelings that led to your behavior. Give yourself credit for being able to learn and grow from the experience as well as for taking steps to be responsible for your actions.

o Accept that you are human and that you will make mistakes.

o If you continue to feel guilty, ask yourself what you are getting out of continuing to beat yourself up. Are you trying to convince others that you are paying for your mistake? Is feeling guilty your way of buying into negative programming about being a bad or undeserving person? Is it your way of not taking responsibility for your actions, making amends and/or changing?

o Forgive yourself and let go. Develop forgiving affirmations like, "I choose to make amends for my mistake and learn from it in the best way I can, and I choose to forgive myself and experience peace." Repeat your forgiveness affirmation until you no longer feel guilty.

Working with Emotions

Emotions are neither good nor bad, they are simply tools to help us interpret what we are experiencing and prepare us for action. They alert us to threats and opportunities in our environment and, as such, prepare us to take necessary action. When we are aware of and in touch with our emotions we can use them to tell us whether our limits and boundaries are being honored and whether our needs are being met. According to John Bradshaw, emotions allow us to monitor our basic needs and give us the power to act.

Once we have tuned into our emotions and learned to use them as tools to getting our needs met, it is important to learn to express and release our emotions in a way that allows us to let go of them. Relaxing our emotions in this way is just as important as relaxing our bodies when it comes to relieving stress. Below are some effective ways to relax emotions.

STRATEGIES

o **Communicate.** Take the time to find a supportive person to share your feelings with. Make sure you let that person know whether you just want him/her to listen or to offer input as well.

o **Cry.** If you are sad, give in to the urge to express your sadness through tears, especially if you have been holding them in for a long time.

o **Journal.** Processing your feelings through writing is a particularly effective way of expressing and releasing your emotions. Not only does it help in making sense of your experience but it provides a record you can refer to as needed when similar feelings come up again.

o **Laugh.** See below.

o **Do something you love.** Doing something you enjoy, like exercising, gardening, reading is as beneficial as laughter.

Laughter

When we are experiencing stress or anxiety it is sometimes hard to find things to laugh about, but laughter truly is good medicine and a great stress reducer. When we laugh, nerves in the brain trigger electrical impulses which stimulate the production of endorphins. As we know, endorphins are hormones which have the ability to calm and relax us, give us a sense of well-being and even alleviate pain. Laughter has been shown to have many other benefits as well, such as aiding digestion, improving blood flow, relieving muscle tension and boosting immunity by helping overcome feelings of panic, anxiety and depression.

STRATEGY

Find out what makes you laugh and then make a plan to create laughter opportunities regularly.

o Buy a book of your favorite comic strip.
o Call dial-a-joke.
o Watch the comedy cable channel.
o Rent your favorite comedy movies.
o Go to a comedy club.
o Go to an amusement park.
o Play a silly game.
o Play a game with children.

○ Spend time with a humorous friend.
○ Compile a notebook of your favorite jokes.
○ Compile a notebook of funny incidents that have occurred to you or others.

Exercise

Researchers have found that exercise can elevate mood, reduce stress and anxiety and improve physical health. Because of these findings, exercise is included as a critical component in many mind/body wellness programs and stress reduction programs such as the Stress Reduction Program at University of Massachusetts Medical Center, the Mind/Body Clinic at Beth Israel Hospital and the Dean Ornish Reversing Heart Disease Program.

Specifically, physical exercise is an important holistic stress management strategy because: 1) it releases the hormones and other by-products that are produced and maintained in the body when the stress response is triggered; 2) it protects against future stress reactivity; and, 3) it releases endorphins which produce positive feelings. Following are important considerations for developing an appropriate exercise program as recommended by experts in the field of stress management:

STRATEGY

○ Consult your primary health care provider before beginning an exercise program, especially if you have any specific health problems or concerns.
○ Choose an activity you enjoy, otherwise you will be less likely to make a commitment to a regular program.
○ Keep in mind that the exercises that are most beneficial for stress prevention and reduction do not involve intense competition or high risk. Avoid any activity that leaves you more tense than when you started; for example, if it upsets you to lose or perform poorly in any particular physical activity do not use this activity as your stress management strategy.
○ In order to maintain fitness it is recommended that you exercise for 20 to 40 minutes per day (depending on the inten-

sity of the activity), three to five times per week. The goal is to increase your heart rate at a comfortable pace which does not interfere with your breathing.

o Allow sufficient time to warm up prior to exercise and cooldown after exercise.

o Wait at least two hours after eating a large meal before exercising. Wait at least one hour after exercising before eating.

o Use appropriate clothing and work-out gear.

o Stop exercising if you experience pain, shortness of breath or any other unusual symptom and consult your health care provider.

o Stick with it. Find ways to motivate and reward yourself.

Improving Your Diet

Our nutrition habits play an important role in managing or exacerbating stress. Certain foods, beverages and drugs may increase stimulation of the stress response and/or deplete important minerals and vitamins which help sustain the body during stress. In 1995 the U.S. Department of Agriculture published the following dietary guidelines.

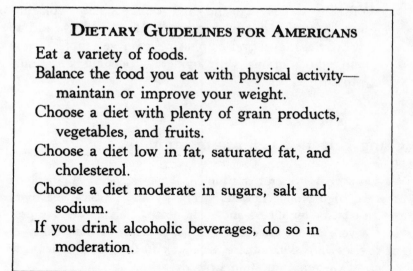

DIETARY GUIDELINES FOR AMERICANS

Eat a variety of foods.

Balance the food you eat with physical activity—
maintain or improve your weight.

Choose a diet with plenty of grain products,
vegetables, and fruits.

Choose a diet low in fat, saturated fat, and
cholesterol.

Choose a diet moderate in sugars, salt and
sodium.

If you drink alcoholic beverages, do so in
moderation.

STRATEGY

Experts in the field of stress management add the following nutritional recommendations:

o Avoid caffeine. It is a stimulant substance which chemically triggers the stress response. Caffeine is found in a variety of beverages and foods including coffee, tea, soda and chocolate. It is also in some headache remedies.

o Vitamins and minerals, especially the B vitamin complex and magnesium, are needed during times of stress. Moreover, certain substances such as caffeine, aspirin, nicotine and alcohol deplete important vitamin and mineral resources. Other refined and processed foods such as white flour, white rice, white sugar, which are stripped of fiber and often made into foods that are laced with preservatives and artificial colorings, provide inadequate nutritional value.

o Caffeine, refined sugars, white flour and alcohol (even in moderation) often lead to symptoms such as anxiety, nervousness, irritability, depression, headache, diarrhea, irregular heartbeat, inability to concentrate and stomach problems.

o Pay close attention to what you eat and drink. Read the labels on all food, beverage and drug packages before consuming them. Gradually remove the foods which add to your stress level and emphasize fresh vegetables, fruits and whole grains with moderate portions of animal protein.

Using Effective Communication

We know that stressful relationships rival smoking, high blood pressure, high blood cholesterol, obesity and physical inactivity as a risk factor for illness and early death. This knowledge provides a very strong incentive for us to improve the quality of our relationships with others. One way to do that is to learn to use effective communication strategies.

STRATEGY I

○ Do not view an argument as a contest to win or lose. When anyone "wins" an argument, everyone loses.

○ In an argument consider that you are both on the same side and the goal is a resolution that both will feel good about.

○ Stick to the subject being discussed.

○ Express your feelings using "I" statements.

○ Avoid starting sentences with "You always" or "You never." These words are guaranteed to put the other person on the defensive and are a set-up for further conflict.

○ In planning what you are going to say to someone, consider how you would like to be spoken to.

○ Make no assumptions or judgments about how the other thinks or feels.

○ Leave people, places and situations that have no present bearing on the subject out of the discussion.

○ Listen to what the other person has to say.

○ Repeat back to the person what you heard him or her say.

○ If a "time out" is requested, make sure you both agree on a "time in" (when you will resume the discussion).

○ Never leave the person you are arguing with until:

1. The argument is resolved or you both agree that a solution cannot be found.
2. A "time out—time in" has been agreed on.
3. You have agreed not to harbor any resentments.

STRATEGY II

The following communication tool can be extremely effective and satisfying to people willing to use it to improve communication. It may feel awkward at first, but if communication creates stress in your relationship, this tool will help you structure your interactions so that each of you is heard and hears the other. Your communication can be significantly less stressful and your level of satisfaction with each other can be significantly improved. Follow these guidelines for better communication:

○ Express how you feel in a given situation and be specific about when and why you feel that way. Just as important, tell your partner, friend or boss what you need.

o The other party repeats the feeling and other information as precisely as possible and says what he/she is willing to do in response to your requested need.
o The dialogue looks like this:

1st person: I feel (mad, sad, glad, afraid), when you _____.
because_____.
What I need from you is_____.

2nd person: What I heard you say is_____.
What I'm willing to do is_____.

---

o The other party then has the opportunity to use the communication tool to express how he feels about that particular situation.
o Once you have agreed to work on an issue together, make sure you agree on how you can tell each other when that issue comes up again. For example, ask the other person, "How can I tell you in a way you can hear, that . . . (you're not listening, you're raising your voice, etc.). In this way you can both agree on how you want to be approached and spoken to about potentially stressful issues.
o Remember to take the opportunity to use this tool to express what's going right with your relationship also—not just what's going wrong!

Building Stress Hardiness

Stress hardiness is a concept developed by Suzanne Kobasa as a result of her extensive research, which showed that the presence or absence of a certain combination of attitudes can be a reliable predictor of whether people under stress get sick or not. The concept of stress hardiness involves a sense of challenge, commitment and control. Challenge is defined as the ability to see life changes and potential stressors as opportunities rather than as threats. Commitment is defined as a sense of one's own involvement and meaning in what is happening in his/her life. Control is defined as the belief that one has influence over his/her life. One way to discover whether these attitudes are operating in your life and to what extent they may be a part of your life is to consider the following:

STRATEGY

Challenge

A sense of challenge speaks directly to our ability to manage stress. When we perceive potential stressors as opportunities we are able to think positively about the challenges they may represent and perhaps even look forward to them. Just as important, a sense of challenge lessens the likelihood that we will trigger the stress response with threatening thoughts. In order to feel a sense of challenge, consider:

o What you have to gain/learn if you succeed.
o What is the worst thing that could happen.
o What your options are.

Control

Identify what you have control over versus what you do not have control over. You *do* have control over:

o What you tell yourself about yourself.
o What you tell yourself about the potential stessor (person, thing, situation, event) you might be exposed to.
o What you feel (because you have control over what you think, you also have control over what you feel).
o How you behave (since thoughts and feelings lead to behaviors, once you are aware of your thoughts and feelings you also have control over your behaviors).
o Seeing choices and options; the more you allow yourself to identify choices and options, the more control you will feel you have, even in situations that are not completely under your control.

You *do not* have control over:

○ What other people say and do, including your spouse, part-
　ner, adult children, friends, coworkers.
○ The weather.

Commitment

We can feel a sense of commitment toward relationships, causes,
animals, spirituality, community, work, hobbies and so on. Consider the following:

○ What areas in your life do you consider worthy of your time,
　effort, attention and resources? These areas represent your
　current commitments.
○ How can you strengthen your commitments?
○ Are there other areas of your life you would like to feel a
　commitment toward? What steps can you take to make
　it happen?

Seeing Options: the Story of Viktor Frankl

The ability to see options and choices is also related to stress
hardiness. When we do not allow our thoughts to include options
we feel trapped. Feeling trapped threatens our ability to adopt
stress-hardy attitudes such as a sense of challenge and control.
When we believe there are no options, it is difficult to look for
opportunities and to exert whatever power we do have in a given
situation. Without a sense of challenge and control, it is even
more difficult to feel commitment or a sense of meaning in life.

Finding meaning in life is the premise of a psychoanalytic
theory developed by psychiatrist Viktor Frankl. Frankl's personal
and professional experiences represent the ultimate strategy for
seeing options and in so doing, to become stress hardy.

In *Man's Search for Meaning*, Frankl tells of his capture and
imprisonment in the death camps of Nazi Germany. He was
stripped of almost everything that had meaning for him. His
father, mother, brother and wife died in the camps or were

gassed, leaving his sister as the only other survivor in the family. Every possession, including his life's work (a manuscript on logotherapy), was taken from him or was destroyed. He was deprived of almost every basic human need during years of suffering from hunger, cold and brutality, including the constant threat of death. Almost every iota of control was taken from him. Even though he was put in charge of the camp infirmary, he was not given access to any medical or nutritional supplies.

Frankl endured and survived the camps because he exercised probably the only option, the only choice, left to him. The one thing that the Nazis could not take from him was the power over his own mind. He used his last vestige of control to choose what he would think about and focus on. He seized every opportunity to choose survival, and he used his spirituality to find meaning in the memory of loved ones and in the beauty of nature.

Frankl and others have found that many survivors of the death camps shared these and other similar qualities. Thankfully, most of us will never have to endure such suffering. With that in mind, it's easier to put our own struggles into perspective. If concentration camp survivors could grasp some sense of what their options were, you certainly can.

STRATEGY

○ Accept the basic premise that there are always options, even if the only option is to change the way you view a situation or circumstance. Look for opportunities rather than threats.

○ Understand that one option is always to do nothing. Electing to do nothing is, however, a choice and that choice may not alleviate your responsibility in a given circumstance.

○ Allow yourself to brainstorm options. Brainstorming involves letting your imagination run free without criticism or judgment, making a list of alternatives and then, with an open mind, evaluating and prioritizing workable ideas.

○ Ask others to suggest possible options, but be careful not to simply accept their suggestions. Making a responsible choice involves validating your options internally, not externally.

Life Planning

Another strategy for ensuring that you are stress hardy is to invest time and effort in planning your life. When you know what your life goals are, you know where you want to go and you can take steps to get there. A life plan is not a static document but a dynamic process through which you can feel a sense of control about what happens in your life, a sense of challenge as you accomplish your goals and a sense of commitment as you allow your goals to have meaning for you.

STRATEGY

○ What do you most want to accomplish in your life? List 10 goals. They may concern relationships, work, money, education, hobbies, spirituality, etc.

○ What do you want your long-term lifestyle to be? List 10 components of your long-term lifestyle. Do you want to work 65 hours a week or 40 hours per week? Do you want time for a hobby, for a relationship, for children/grandchildren?

○ Prioritize each of your two lists—life accomplishment goals and lifestyle goals—by order of importance.

○ Examine and reconcile your priorities. Are your life accomplishment goals in tune with your lifestyle goals? For example, if having money is a top priority for you and you work 65 hours a week to get it, does this support or conflict with your lifestyle goals?

○ Once you have reconciled your priorities, take each goal and develop an action plan to reach that goal. Identify the resources you will need (who, what, when). Write out the steps that need to be taken. Take action. Evaluate the results. Make adjustments as needed.

o This exercise is most effective when it is used as a dynamic tool. Make the time to reassess your goals at regular intervals. Use this time to make any necessary modifications and to reaffirm your commitment to these life and life-style goals.

o Remember that movement toward a goal is just as important as achieving it.

o If you have a life partner, be sure to share your goals with him or her. Ask your life partner to do this exercise and then compare notes. Consider whether any of your goals support or are in conflict with your partner's goals.

Overcoming Struggle

The following story illustrates the ways in which we choose to see situations and sometimes, the way we respond to life in general.

> Three men working side by side at the task of laying bricks are asked what they are doing. The first man answers angrily, "I'm laying bricks—what does it look like I'm doing?" The second man, replies with a heavy sigh, "I'm earning a living." The third man says with conviction, "I'm building a cathedral."

How do you respond to specific tasks and to life in general? Are you able to see the opportunities and respond with enthusiasm to situations you find yourself in or do you find yourself struggling through each day?

The truth is, many of us create or choose to struggle when we don't have to. Let's look at some of the reasons we struggle.

1. Struggle is an automatic response. We simply respond with our negative programming about struggle: "No pain, no gain. There are no free rides in life—you have to pay your dues. You have to struggle in order to be worthy of getting into heaven." Our programming eliminates the need to think and becomes an automatic response.

2. Struggle validates that we shouldn't have expectations or desires. Then we won't be disappointed or look foolish to others. In the same way, struggle validates self-doubt and saves us from taking risks and not succeeding.

3. Struggle gives us a sense of meaning and worth when we don't know any other way to find these values. This is especially true when we're afraid of succeeding or actually getting what we want, or when we feel that, in some way, we don't deserve it. "I'm *supposed* to struggle to get to heaven." "If I don't struggle there will be no reward." We often respond to this sense of undeservability by becoming enmeshed in some form of struggle, so instead of focusing on our goal or what we desire, we focus on our fear, anger, hurt, loneliness, self-pity or despair in order to give us a sense of worth or meaning.

4. Struggle gives us a sense of entitlement. "If I struggle this hard, regardless of the quality of my effort, I deserve something in return."

5. Struggle is what some people use to feel alive. When we're not comfortable with, or used to feeling happy, struggle—however negative—can give us a sense of passion, an adrenaline hit, a feeling of being real. When we depend on struggle for these feelings, struggle becomes an addiction.

6. Struggle allows us to keep old wounds alive, almost as if letting go of the struggle would make the wound less real or meaningful.

The bottom line is that we struggle because we get something out of it. For many of us, actually succeeding, or getting what we desire is just too threatening. We all know someone who seems to have it all—the house, the relationship, the money, the kids, the job, the friends. But instead of celebrating those things, they find something to complain about or to worry about. It's never quite enough.

Maybe it's because people find it easier to commiserate together, perhaps misery really does love company. Maybe it's because we're just scared to be too happy because we've been programmed to believe that happiness can't last and something bad will come along to ruin it. So instead, we make struggle the main issue instead of focusing on being grateful for what we have or finding a solution to whatever problem may be at hand.

STRATEGY

○ Reflect on the role of struggle in your life and look for alternatives to struggle.

○ Review "Seeing Options" for help in looking for alternatives.

○ Consider this question: *What if our purpose is to learn to enjoy life?* How would your response to life change if you programmed yourself with beliefs like: "I am worthy and deserving of having a happy life." Or, "My purpose in life is to experience as much awe, wonder and joy as possible."

Loving Detachment

Loving detachment is a strategy that is particularly effective when dealing with issues of control and codependency. Detaching does not mean we do not care. It means we learn to love and care without becoming so enmeshed with other people that we do not see our own limits and boundaries. *Codependency No More* author Melodie Beattie describes the rewards of detachment as serenity, a deep sense of peace, the ability to give and receive love in self-enhancing, energizing ways, the freedom to find real solutions to our problems and the freedom to live our own lives without excessive feelings of guilt about, or responsibility toward, others.

STRATEGY

One of the most effective ways to accomplish loving detachment is to adopt the following attitudes:

○ I detach from others knowing that I care about them and what happens to them, but that I am not responsible for them nor is it my responsibility to control them.

○ Every person is responsible for his own thoughts, feelings and behaviors.

○ It is not my responsibility to solve the problems of others.

○ Since it is not my responsibility to solve the problems of others, then worrying about those problems does not help.

○ This frees me to take control of my own problems and take action to solve them.

○ By detaching from others I allow them the freedom to take responsibility for their own problems and to grow from doing so.

Self-Acceptance

As we know already, various events, circumstances and people in our environment can act as triggers to stress, but ultimately, the most important component of stress is what we tell ourselves about ourselves—whether that trigger represents an opportunity or a threat to us. When we tell ourselves negative messages about a potential stressor such as, "I can't handle it, I'm unworthy or undeserving. There's something wrong with me, I'm not okay the way I am," we will see that potential stressor as a threat and experience stress. When we threaten ourselves in this way, we cut ourselves off from a loving relationship with ourselves and therefore we damage our spiritual connection with ourselves.

Stop for a moment and consider the words, "I am okay the way I am." Now watch for your next thought. Chances are, if you are experiencing a lot of stress, you are telling yourself, in some way, that you are not okay. Maybe your thought is some variation of, "I'm okay the way I am, but I could be much better," or "I'm okay, but I still have a long way to go," or "I'm not okay, look at how much better everyone else is than me." These messages are an indication that we are criticizing, evaluating and/or judging ourselves. In other words, we are not accepting ourselves.

How can we accept ourselves just the way we really are in the moment, especially when it seems obvious that we need to change? For some of us, depending on our childhood and other programming, self-acceptance may feel like giving up striving for a better life. Or, it may feel like overindulging or coddling ourselves, or even denying what it is we need to change in our lives.

Self-acceptance as I define it is *the ability to accept oneself in the moment with compassion and without self-criticism, self-evaluation or self-judgment.*

STRATEGY

○ The first step toward self-acceptance is learning to get in touch with your feelings and your needs. This often requires dispelling the myth that some feelings, like anger and sadness, are bad or that you are not worthy of other feelings like happiness. Remember, feelings are neither good nor bad; they are essential tools for identifying our needs and getting them met. In order to truly experience self-acceptance it is essential to learn to honor and respect your feelings while at the same time letting them flow naturally, not denying them, stuffing them or otherwise distracting yourself from them.

○ The second step is to let go of the idea that the only way to grow and change is through pain and hard work. With your mind open to the idea that there may be an easier, less stressful way of living, you can stop putting yourself down and begin to affirm, "I'm okay the way I am."

○ The third step is to create affirmations which reflect your new openness. "I accept myself in this present moment, without self-criticism, self-judgment or self-evaluation, knowing that I am continuing to work on myself and do better."

○ If and when you slip back into beating yourself up, allow yourself to become aware of it, to stop those thoughts and to replace them with self-acceptance affirmations.

○ As you learn to accept yourself, you will experience longer and longer periods of feeling that you truly are okay. When you reach this stage you will also experience inner peace.

Self-Compassion

Self-Acceptance and Self-Compassion are similar strategies which aid us in attaining and maintaining our spiritual connection with ourselves. I define self-compassion as *the ability to identify with one's own suffering and the desire to relieve it through loving and caring acts.*

Just as with self-acceptance, self-compassion does not mean we do not intend to work on our shortcomings, it just means that we are able to love ourselves as we are in the present moment, and that we are granting ourselves the same kind of compassion we so easily feel and offer to others that we love.

The feelings of being unworthy or undeserving of happiness translate into a lack of love for ourselves. As a result of these feelings, we find it incredibly difficult to feel compassion for ourselves. We monitor, we judge and we boss ourselves mercilessly. But when we are able to be compassionate with ourselves, even for a moment, we learn to observe ourselves in the moment with an attitude of love and care.

Most importantly, when we come from a place of compassion for ourselves we can free up all the energy we put into self-criticism, self-evaluation and self-judgment; redirect it into accepting those areas in ourselves that need work and compassionately begin to do the work. Another advantage is that we have more energy to put into living more fully and more consciously in the present moment.

STRATEGY

The next time you find yourself being critical or hard on yourself:

o Imagine that someone you love or care about—a special friend, spouse, child—was being as hard on him/herself as you are being toward yourself. What would you tell them? Would you say something like, "It's okay to make mistakes, You don't have to be perfect to be loved and accepted, You're a good person." Try reflecting those words and compassionate feelings back to yourself now. In this way you can learn to be more affectionate and gentle with yourself.

○ Picture yourself as a small child at the youngest age you can remember. Visualize your child-self (often referred to as your inner child) as clearly as possible, then send feelings of love and compassion to that small child. In your mind's eye, see yourself hugging your child-self. If feelings or thoughts other than love and compassion enter, gently return your mind to thoughts of love and compassion. Practice this compassion exercise recalling other images of yourself through childhood, adolescence and eventually adulthood.

○ Keep trying these exercises even if it feels difficult. Keep in mind that it will get easier in time.

Self-Love

Learning to love ourselves and keeping that love alive is truly a life-long process. Certainly there is no single strategy that can lead us to love ourselves, but certain practices such as self-acceptance and self-compassion are practical first steps in that direction. Consider the following strategies as ways to deepen your self-love.

STRATEGY I

○ Ask yourself these questions:

How do you know when you are loving yourself?

What thoughts, actions or other tools do you use to practice self-love?

What are the signs or "red flags" that tell you that you are not being self-loving?

In what areas of your life is it easiest to practice self-love (relationships with spouse, children, other family, friends; job; community work; body image)?

In what areas of your life is it most difficult to practice self-love?

What would be different if you were able to practice more self-love, even in those areas where you find it most difficult?

What is it that you need to do to be more self-loving?

O Think about someone you love unconditionally, even a pet! How do you treat that person or pet? How do you speak to and act around this individual? Why is it easy to love this being unconditionally? Use this information to learn unconditionally loving ways to treat and talk to yourself.

O What makes you unique? Explore your talents and abilities. Identify your attributes and personality traits. These are some of the qualities that make you unique. Don't let false modesty get in the way, just be as honest and objective as possible. Practice embracing your uniqueness and loving yourself because you are unique.

O Self-love affirmations are very powerful. Make them part of your daily self-talk. You can use the examples below but I also encourage you to create affirmations that are unique and meaningful to you.

I love myself unconditionally.

I'm as compassionate with myself as I am with other people.

I am a good person and I'm coming from a place of good intention.

I am worthy and deserving of happiness.

I love and respect all my natural abilities.

I love my uniqueness.

I love and accept my (all the things you can't change about yourself) hair, eyes, ears, feet, voice, accent, laugh, etc.

I am able to let go of judging myself and others.

As a human being, I accept my mistakes and use them as opportunities for personal and spiritual growth.

God (or, fill in your own word) loves me.

STRATEGY II

This strategy and the one that follows have been very powerful self-love tools for me and many of my clients. For those who are comfortable with them, these strategies are also very powerful tools to achieve inner peace.

It is particularly comforting to believe in a Divine power that is unconditionally loving and compassionate. Allow yourself to focus on the affirmation:

> God (or fill in your own word) loves me unconditionally and compassionately.

Say it to yourself with as much meaning as possible. Now allow yourself to reflect on what it means to you to be loved without condition for who you are as a person, not for what you do; loved for your uniqueness. Feel your Divine power understands everything about you, including your struggles and accomplishments.

As you reflect, consider that each time you judge yourself harshly, abuse yourself in some way or fail to forgive yourself, you are denigrating God's love for you. In this sense, when you are not practicing self-love, you are disrespecting your Higher Power. The more you reflect on the belief that God loves you unconditionally and expects you to love yourself that same way, the easier it is to feel it.

STRATEGY III

Imagine a channel of loving energy opening from your heart and being directed toward the heavens, to your image of a Divine or Higher power. See your image of a Divine power returning loving energy to you. Become aware of the flow of that energy back and forth. Notice how easy or difficult it is for you to experience love for yourself and love for your Divine power. On what level or to what extent can you experience this love. For example: "It feels okay to think of God loving me as a member of the human race, but not as an individual." Or, "it feels okay to let Divine love in when I feel good about myself but not when I feel bad about myself." If it's hard for you to feel your own self-love or a Higher power's love for you, it's usually a sign that you are not loving yourself unconditionally.

Practice letting loving energy flow back and forth between you and your Divine power until it becomes easy and effortless.

Living in the Present Moment: the #1 Stress Reducer

Worry and guilt create a tremendous amount of stress. Yet, we waste an incredible amount of our time feeling guilty about the past and worrying about the future instead of focusing on living in the present moment. Living in the present moment is the number-one stress management strategy because when we allow ourselves to put all our cognitive, emotional, physical and spiritual energy into being in the here and now, it prevents us from feeling guilty about the past or worrying about the future. Although we have already mentioned some of the following strategies, it is worthwhile to refer to them here in the context of this discussion.

STRATEGY

o In order to be in the present moment learn to be aware of what you are thinking, feeling and doing. Healing breath work and meditation are very effective in helping to develop this kind of awareness. Meditation and relaxation also fine-tune the ability to focus and concentrate on one thing at a time and to quiet the negative self-talk that leads to guilt and worry.

o Once you develop your capacity for awareness, focus and concentration, use these tools to become fully engaged and absorbed in the task or situation you are experiencing in the moment. In other words, consciously choose to let go of guilt and worry and experience the peace that comes from being in the present.

o Use Healing Breath Work and Mind/Body Checks to focus on what is happening in your mind and body at any particular moment in time and in so doing, bring yourself back to the present moment if you have drifted into the past or the future.

○ Use the Living in the Present Moment Strategy to find sub-
stantive meaning in your life and activities. You cannot
control the past, but you do have a certain amount of
control over the present. Many of your actions in the
present influence your future. Since you cannot relive the
past and since there are no guarantees about the future,
the only real point of power is in the here and now.

○ Watch a child or kitten at play for a powerful lesson in living
in the present moment. When a child discovers a new
object, like a stone, he/she uses all the senses to explore
it—smelling it, touching it, looking at it, tasting it, shak-
ing it for a sound to listen to. A kitten, on the other hand,
can turn a paper bag into a hiding place or a ball of string
into a toy. In both cases, the focus is completely with the
object or task at hand without judgment, concern or
limits.

Gratitude

Gratitude is a great stress reducer because it keeps us in the
present moment. Gratitude motivates us to focus on what we
have to be thankful for instead of wallowing in what is wrong
with our lives. When we allow ourselves to focus on what we
are thankful for in our lives we are focusing on positive, here-
and-now thoughts as opposed to guilty feelings about the past
and worried feelings about the future.

The more we practice gratitude, the more we focus on opportunities rather than on threats. When we are focused on opportunities we are telling ourselves that we are able to cope with what
life presents us. The result is that we are far less likely to experience stress and anxiety. When we take the time to be grateful it
becomes an exercise in spirituality because it is difficult to be truly
thankful for something that we do not feel a connection with.

STRATEGY

○ Make time to practice moments of gratitude often and regularly each day, perhaps starting each morning before you

get out of bed. During those moments allow yourself to become aware of all those things in your life that you appreciate and that you are thankful for—your talents, abilities and senses; friends, children and loved ones; the food you eat; the music you hear; other people who work to provide you with food, music, etc.; animals, flowers, birds, trees, the sun, the sky, the ocean and all of nature. There is nothing too small or too large that is not worthy of our gratitude.

o Make time to remember and be thankful for people you have come in contact with in your life who have treated you with kindness and consideration, whether in word or deed.

o Make time to remember and appreciate people who may not have treated you with kindness or consideration, but who may have contributed to your personal growth nonetheless. For example, the coach or teacher who may have taught you a skill by pushing you hard or criticizing you.

o Allow yourself to become aware of how gratitude affects you. As you continue to practice gratitude, you will find that you have less and less reason to feel sad, depressed or resentful and more reason to feel positive and to look for the opportunities life has to offer.

Wonder

The *American Heritage Dictionary* defines *wonder* as something "that arouses awe, astonishment, surprise, curiosity or admiration." Wonder is the key to letting go of stagnation and negativity in our lives. Like gratitude, it keeps us in the present moment. It allows us to open to miracles and synchronicities. It puts us back in touch with the magic of living. It means opening to whatever you're experiencing in the present moment, even if you've done, seen or thought the same thing a thousand times before.

STRATEGY

o Find one thing to be in wonder about every day. Consider animals, nature, the human body, the human spirit, chil-

dren at play, mechanical things, food, sunlight, the sky, plants, birds, buildings, a beautiful piece of music.
o Practice bringing the focus of your attention to whatever you are doing or experiencing. Then, try to find something wondrous or surprising about it.

Listening to Your Inner Voice

Have you ever had a "gut" feeling or intuition about something—ignored it—and then regretted it? Why do we ignore our intuition when we could develop it and put it to good use? Whatever your reasons may be, here are some ideas about how you can foster this very special human gift.

There is a calm, peaceful place inside of us that knows all we need to know to make sound decisions for ourselves. This place, our intuition, is also often referred to as our inner voice or higher self. We access our inner voice by quieting our minds, stopping the internal self-talk, and going inside ourselves through the process of meditation or relaxation. When we are in touch with our higher self or inner voice we are able to find answers to questions or problems via a deep-felt sense of knowing. This knowing is sometimes referred to as an "Aha!" experience, a gut feeling or an intuitive sense. It is the ultimate form of internal validation, allowing us to look to ourselves, rather than to others, to decide what we think, believe and feel.

One way to tune in to our inner voice is to learn to trust the wisdom of our bodies. This is sometimes referred to as kinesthetic wisdom. We have learned to tune out the wisdom of our bodies by going numb to our feelings or focusing on external influences such as others' needs or expectations of us. Sometimes we are influenced by the guilt imposed on us by others or by our desire to be liked, not judged or criticized. At other times, our fear of making others angry or of being different influences us. By focusing on these external cues and not listening to our own internal cues, we often are not able to determine what is in our own best interest.

We were all born with the inherent capacity to know at every given moment in time exactly what is best for us. We simply need to reclaim that skill. Our bodies and our minds are linked by a complex system of neurological and physiological connections. As a result, when we learn to tune in to our mind/body we can tune in to the unique knowledge it has to offer us about ourselves.

Before using either of the following strategies, allow yourself to quiet your internal self-talk and to relax your body with a brief meditation, relaxation or a few healing breaths.

STRATEGY I

Once relaxed, simply call to mind the problem or concern and ask yourself what feels right. Then be open to an answer in whatever form it comes. The answer may come in the form of words, it may come in the form of an image or it may come as a deep sense of inner knowing.

STRATEGY II

1. Write down the problem or concern and then list as many possible solutions as you can.

2. Then, focus on your body and its sensations for a moment. Scan your body briefly from head to toe and become aware of what feelings and sensations may be present so that you can later make note of any changes.

3. Next, close your eyes and repeat to yourself one of the solutions you developed, be still and note any changes in your body awareness. It is essential that you clear your mind of any self-talk during the process and key in solely to your bodily reactions. Do your muscles tighten or relax? Do you feel a sense of physical discomfort like burning, or physical relief like warmth or glowing?

4. Go through steps 2 and 3 for each possible solution. Cross out solutions that stimulate negative reactions and circle those that stimulate positive reactions.

5. If there is more than one solution that generates a positive response, repeat the process again just for the positive ones and determine which one generates the strongest positive response.

Volunteering

Volunteering not only reduces stress but makes us healthier physically, emotionally and spiritually. Allan Luks and Peggy Payne report that 95 percent of the 3,300 people they surveyed had experienced a "helper's high" after volunteering. Respondents compared their helper's high to drug and alcohol-induced euphoria, runner's high, orgasm and the tranquility induced by yoga. Volunteers also reported experiencing a stronger sense of connection with other people as well as sensations of mastery, challenge, optimism, joy and control. In fact, 57 percent mentioned an increased sense of self-worth, and 53 percent noted gains in happiness and optimism. This calming sensation can have lifelong benefits in counteracting loneliness, depression, hostility and helplessness.

According to the survey, volunteering not only brings about a sense of greater emotional and spiritual well-being but also can improve physical health. Volunteers said that helping others has helped them maintain good health and diminish symptoms of chronic disease, especially those involving physical pain. Nine out of ten respondents who experienced "helper's high" rated their health as better than that of other people their age.

STRATEGY

According to the Luks and Payne survey, the most beneficial types of volunteering include the following components:

○ Enjoyment in what you are doing.
○ Personal contact with people.
○ Frequency—approximately two hours per week.
○ Helping strangers as opposed to family and friends (leads to the strongest helper's high).

o Volunteering in a supportive organization.
o Utilizing skills you have confidence in.
o Making an emotional and physical effort.
o Letting go of expectations.

Inner Peace

Some guidelines for knowing when you are well on the road to achieving inner peace:

o You regard unexpected events, circumstances, people and conditions in your life as opportunities rather than as threats.
o You begin to believe in your ability to cope with just about anything life has to offer.
o You stop thinking negatively about yourself.
o You stop thinking negatively about others.
o You begin to know what your needs are and are successful at getting them met.
o You stop feeling unnecessarily guilty and worried.
o You find yourself feeling connected to others and to all things in the universe.
o You find yourself spontaneously feeling grateful.
o You listen to your inner voice for answers about what's right for you.
o You begin to enjoy each present moment as it is occurring.
o You engage in the wonder of all that life has to offer.

Congratulations! You have arrived.

Overcoming Panic Attacks
without Medication

If you experience intense periods of fear or anxiety that seem to come over you without warning and last for a few moments to a half hour, you may be one of the estimated 10 to 20 million Americans who experience anxiety or panic attacks. These attacks are generally characterized by heart palpitations (sometimes described as a racing, pounding heart or chest discomfort), dizziness and sensations of suffocating. Other symptoms include:

- trembling
- sweating
- diarrhea
- nausea
- restlessness
- hot and cold flashes
- nervousness, agitation
- disorientation
- feelings of helplessness
- panic
- scary, uncontrollable thoughts
- fatigue
- muscle tension
- migraines/headaches
- numbness or tingling
- overwhelming negative thoughts

Many people view the use of antidepressant and antianxiety medications as "magic pills" or an "instant fix" for their panic attacks. But taking medication for panic attacks is like having your foot on the brake and the gas pedal at the same time. You still have the symptoms but your senses are dulled to them.

If you experience panic attacks you should know that there are safe and effective alternatives to medication. Antidepressant and antianxiety medications are not for everyone; not everyone wants to or needs to take a pill to control anxiety attacks, nor is it in their best interest to do so. Psychiatric drugs can be both psychologically and physically addicting and can produce serious side effects, including symptoms of panic and anxiety.

For the most part, drugs do not eliminate panic attacks, they simply numb you to their intensity. The bottom line: you still have panic attacks. You have the pills, but no coping skills. And sometimes, reliance on the pills creates a phobic and/or addictive reaction. Some people are afraid to go anywhere without their pills or are afraid to give up their pills even when they have stopped being effective.

Fortunately, there is a safe and effective way to overcome panic attacks. Research shows that when medication is prescribed to people for panic attacks without psychotherapy, 70 to 90 percent will relapse and have more severe episodes within two months. On the other hand, cognitive therapy approaches alone have proven to be more effective, with relapse rates as low as 0 percent after two years.

The approach I have developed for panic attacks incorporates successful methods from cognitive therapy as well as my personal mind/body/spirit strategies. Nearly 100 percent of the clients I see for panic attacks are able to overcome their attacks without medication within several days to several weeks. This is true even in cases where people have experienced severe trauma or have experienced panic attack symptoms for 20 years or longer. Some people never have another panic attack once they begin using my approach. If you know or suspect you suffer from panic attacks and wish to overcome them without medication, please note that you may need the support of a trained health care or mental health care professional to support you through the process.

First, See Your Health Care Practitioner

Some medical conditions have associated symptoms that are similar to those of a panic attack. For all my clients who are experiencing physical symptoms, I always recommend a thorough examination with a health care professional to rule out any medical condition that may be causing their anxiety symptoms.

Drug-related symptoms

Be aware that use, abuse and/or withdrawal from drugs can lead to symptoms associated with anxiety and panic attacks. In this context, drugs refer to central nervous system stimulants and depressants (including psychiatric medications), alcohol, nicotine and caffeine. As mentioned earlier, antidepressant and antianxiety medications can create the very symptoms they are supposed to alleviate.

If you are on medication for panic attacks, you *must* consult your physician before stopping the medication. Failure to reduce drug dosages properly can lead to withdrawal symptoms.

How Panic Attacks Occur

Before we move directly into the strategy for overcoming panic attacks, there are a few important points to keep in mind.

1. Panic attacks are not a function of the physical symptoms (shortness of breath, heart palpitations, dizziness) that you experience. These attacks are a function of how you *perceive* these symptoms. Like stress, panic attacks are a function of what you tell yourself about yourself, the situation you find yourself in, and your ability to cope with the symptoms you experience. People who have panic attacks tell themselves that the symptoms are, in some way, a threat to them. The bottom line is that they engage in distorted thinking by misinterpreting the symptoms and assuming catastrophic results. People often tell themselves some version of the following distorted thoughts:

o This will never end. I'll always feel like this.
o I am losing control.
o I will make a fool out of myself.
o I'm dying.
o I'm choking.
o I'm going to pass out.
o I'm having a heart attack.
o I can't catch my breath.
o I'm going to hurt myself (or someone else).
o I'm going crazy. I'm losing my mind.
o I have no control over this.
o Something is terribly wrong with me.

2. If you are truly experiencing a panic attack and your health care practitioner has ruled out any underlying medical condition, understand that your thinking is distorted for the following reasons:

o Panic attacks activate the fight/flight or stress response. When the stress response is triggered intensely enough, as it is during a panic attack, certain physiological changes occur in the body which are responsible for most of the symptoms noted earlier.
o While panic attacks are extremely painful and terrifying, no one has ever died from one.
o I have never known anyone to pass out as a result of a panic attack. This is because panic activates the stress response which raises the heart rate and blood pressure. In order to pass out, heart rate and blood pressure must drop quickly or significantly.
o Panic attacks *do* end. For the most part, they last from several seconds to 15–30 minutes or so.
o I have never known people to lose control, make a fool of themselves, hurt themselves or others or go crazy during a panic attack. They may find it necessary to leave the room or space they are in or even pull over to the side of the road if driving, but these are rational behaviors under the circumstances. As you become comfortable with the strategy described later in this chapter, you will learn to feel confident that you *can* control panic attacks and eliminate them.
o There is nothing terribly wrong with you and you are not

losing your mind. Millions of people experience panic attacks. It is simply your body's way of reacting to your mind's messages.

3. Panic attacks are brought on by negative thoughts about a potential stressor and are simply an extreme form of the stress response. If we modify the Stress Response Profile (see page 85) to fit a panic attack scenario, panic and/or anxiety is the unhealthy behavior that results.

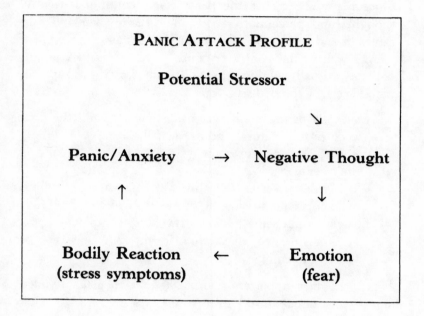

We know that potential triggers or stressors can be situations, events, people or conditions. Most often we think of stressors as being outside of ourselves. In the case of panic attacks, we can also specify that what is happening inside of us, that is, our bodily sensations, can also be potential stressors. So panic attacks can be triggered in one of two ways:

1. Negative thoughts about a situation, event, person or condition.
   o   I'm afraid of driving (in general, over bridges, on the highway).
   o   I'm afraid of closed spaces.
   o   I'm afraid of crowds.

○ What if I panic while I'm (speaking, in the car, at the grocery store).

2. Negative thoughts about bodily sensations.
   ○ This shortness of breath sensation means I'm (choking, dying, having a heart attack).
   ○ This dizzy sensation means I have a brain tumor (there is something terribly wrong with me).
   ○ I'm sweating, I feel nauseous and dizzy, I must be losing control.

3. Once a person reaches the panic stage, continued negative thoughts and perceptions about the situation we find ourselves in and/or our panicky sensations sustain the feeling of fear as well as the body's response to fear—*until* something happens (usually within 15 to 30 minutes) to disrupt the panic cycle. Typical disruptions are:

   ○ The body or the mind becomes exhausted, and the cycle comes to a natural end or we fall asleep,
   ○ We get distracted in some way (child care, cooking or television becomes the focus of our attention).
   ○ We numb ourselves in some way (by eating, drinking alcohol, taking drugs).
   ○ The situation ends (your travel is completed, your mother-in-law leaves, you finish your speech, you leave the store).

4. This is the most important point: *You have the power to interrupt a panic attack at any point in the cycle.*

By using the strategy below you can learn healthy ways to interrupt the panic cycle. As you begin to feel confident in your ability to control an attack, the panic cycles will diminish in frequency and duration until they end completely. For most people, this process can be as short as several days to just a few weeks. Some people find that simply having knowledge about panic attacks and knowing that they have the tools to cope with one if it comes on is enough to prevent them from ever having another one.

Controlling and Eliminating Panic Attacks

STRATEGY

At first glance it might be hard for someone experiencing the frightening and intense symptoms of a panic attack to believe that overcoming them is as simple as the method described below.

Remember that the treatment does not have to be as painful or difficult as the illness. The simplicity of this strategy in no way negates the terror or the life disruptions you may have experienced because of panic attacks. This method is firmly based on proven cognitive therapy treatment protocols, and it works. My overwhelming success with clients proves that it does. (See the success stories about Ann and Sam in Chapter 14.) For those of you who want more detailed information, I have provided several excellent references in the Notes section for this chapter.

My approach to dealing with panic attacks consists of 1) following the Daily Program and 2) a specific strategy to use when experiencing a panic attack.

Daily program

Follow the Daily Program outlined on page 93, especially the following practices:

1. Every hour use diaphragmatic breathing, the body scan and affirmations for one to three minutes.

2. Meditate or use a relaxation tape for 15 to 20 minutes every day. By doing these two things you not only practice diaphragmatic breathing so you are comfortable doing it when you need it the most, you allow your body to stay relaxed and in balance so the chances of having another attack are reduced significantly.

During a panic attack

1. With your new understanding of panic attacks, recognize and accept the fact that you are experiencing an attack. Don't try to fight it or ignore it. Know that you have the tools to cope with it.

2. Breathe! Breathing diaphragmatically will help bring your mind and body back to balance. Such breathing, along with positive self-talk, are the strongest tools you have to interrupt a panic attack at any point in the cycle. The more you have practiced diaphragmatic breathing ahead of time, the easier it will be for you to stop an attack the moment you become aware of one coming on.

3. Keep breathing as you remind yourself that
   o This is just your body's way of reacting to negative thoughts (even if you aren't aware of what those thoughts are).
   o This will pass; it always does.
   o Nothing bad will happen to you.

4. Use your affirmations and positive self-talk, such as: "I am in control of my mind, my emotions and my body. My breathing is deep and regular. Tension melts away with each relaxed breath."

5. Practice being compassionate with yourself and eliminating negative self-talk.

6. If you still feel uncomfortable, meditate, put on a relaxation tape, or become absorbed in an activity.

7. Once the attack has passed, see if you can figure out what triggered it. Were you distorting your thinking in any way? Do you have a need that isn't being met? If so, take steps to get that need met. Please note, however, that *it is* not *necessary to know what triggers your attacks in order to eliminate them.*

   To recap, the key steps are:

   o Knowledge: you have control over your anxiety/panic attacks.
   o Diaphragmatic breathing.
   o This is simply your body's reaction to your mind's messages.
   o It will pass.
   o Positive self-talk.

As you begin to practice these steps you will feel more confident in your ability to control your anxiety. This will empower you. The more empowered you feel, the less opportunity you have to feel anxious or trigger a panic attack.

12

"Yes, but . . ."
Overcoming Resistance to Change

Many of us have a myriad of excuses for not making healthy changes in our lives. Most of these excuses come in the form of "yes, but" statements. "Yes, but I don't have enough time to learn how to manage my stress. Yes, but it's really not *that* bad. Yes, but it's too difficult. Yes, but it's easier just to take a pill. Yes, but I don't have any control over the things that are stressing me out. Yes, but I'm too stressed to manage my stress."

Some of us resist changing our negative behaviors because we feel more comfortable with the status quo. Even though we might experience stress as a result of these behaviors, at least it's something we know and understand. Our habits—and their stressful outcomes—seem normal, natural and safe. Rather than change our behavior, we engage in:

○ **Negative thinking.** "It won't work for me. I'll never be able to learn how. People don't change. I can't change."
○ **Procrastination.** "I'll start tomorrow. I'll start when you start. I'll start when I have more time. I'll start when I feel less stressed. I'll start any time but right now."
○ **Thinking too much.** Analysis leads to paralysis. If we spend all of our time analyzing and intellectualizing about mak-

ing a change, there is often no time left to actually take
action and make the change.

o **Not putting yourself first.** "It's selfish to put myself first
or to take time for myself. I don't have time for myself."

While it may be difficult to imagine that you resist change
because you actually get something out of your negative behavior, it is worth considering. You may be using unhealthy behaviors as a means of fulfilling needs that you don't otherwise know
how to fill. For example:

o **Feeling loved/cared for by others.** For those of us who
always seem to be stressed or in a crisis, staying stressed
may be a means of getting attention from a loved one.

o **Not taking responsibility.** If you get others to do what you
want them to do or what you don't want to do yourself,
you don't have to make decisions or be held accountable for
the consequences. The problem with this behavior is that
often when we don't accept responsibility for ourselves or
exert our own personal power, we can easily become victims.

o **Not accepting and loving yourself.** If you opt for being
stressed and anxious much of the time, you avoid learning
what your needs are and working to get them met. Often
we avoid "going inside" and getting to know ourselves
because we fear we will find out something bad about
ourselves—perhaps that our negative beliefs about being
unworthy and undeserving are true.

In looking at the reasons we might be resisting change, we
must also resist the urge to use that awareness and understanding
to sabotage ourselves. Instead of fueling negative self-talk that
can perpetuate our resistance, we can use the information to seek
out healthier alternatives.

Many people commit themselves to change only after experiencing a physical or emotional crisis of one kind or another. This
is most often when people become "teachable." In other words,
they become willing to make changes after being scared into it,
such as after a heart attack, being arrested for drunk driving or
developing panic attacks. Others simply reach their limit and

become angry or frustrated enough to want to change. Often the impetus for change comes when people feel they are doing too much, not being appreciated or sacrificing their own needs for those of others. Still others contemplate change when they feel trapped or forced to change, as is often the case when a person loses a job or a spouse or a partner threatens to leave a relationship.

While these situations create a motivation for change, *"You don't have to be sick to get better"* as self-help guru Wayne Dyer says. Rather than waiting for a crisis to motivate us, it is possible to exercise our personal power and choose to change *before* a crisis occurs. It is important to remember that the times we need stress management strategies the most are the times when we are least able to use them. This is because our minds and bodies are already in overdrive as the stress response kicks in and, under these circumstances, we are more likely to rely on old, unhealthy habits as coping mechanisms.

To manage stress effectively, it is critical to commit yourself to learning and practicing the recommended strategies *before* you experience stress so that they can become the foundation of new, healthy coping mechanisms. Choosing to make holistic stress management strategies a part of your daily life helps to ensure that you can exercise control in a healthy way, by 1) taking responsibility for those things which are under your control and, 2) managing your reactions to things you do not have control over.

Take this opportunity to overcome whatever resistance you might have to learning the strategies in this book. The first step is to take some action. Begin by setting aside a few minutes today to try one strategy. Keep practicing it, even if it feels awkward at first. All new skills take time to learn and feel comfortable doing. Once you've started, don't turn back. Do not fall into the trap of beating yourself up for not using the strategies, even if you forget or choose not to use them for a while. Remember, the past is already gone, the future has not yet occurred. What we do have is the strength of the present moment to create change. The point of power is now. Take it!

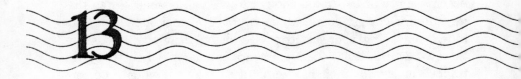

Self-Responsibility: Tapping into Your Personal Power

Self-responsibility can be defined in many ways, but regardless of its definition it is a key ingredient in how you manage stress in your life. In this context, self-responsibility represents your ability to make choices about your thoughts and subsequently to make changes in your life that will positively affect your health and well-being. And when you make these kinds of positive changes you are taking responsibility for yourself and tapping into your own personal power in a way no one else can.

Our health and well-being can be affected by learned attitudes and beliefs concerning control, self-efficacy, optimism and finding meaning in life. These kinds of attitudes are fundamental to the concept of self-responsibility. Self-responsibility also refers to your ability to tap into your own personal power to effect choice and change in your life. Taking charge of your life and using your personal power are critical ingredients in committing to and realizing the benefits of a holistic stress management approach to health and well-being.

When it comes to managing stress, self-responsibility is important whether our stress is a result of our perceptions or physical conditions. For example, we are each responsible for the lifestyle choices we make that disrupt the body's homeostasis and trigger the stress response. These choices can range from deciding what you will put into your body such as drugs, food, water, nicotine, caffeine or alcohol, to how much exercise and sleep you get, to what environmental conditions you expose yourself to (pollution, toxins, radiation, noise, bad weather).

Even when self-responsibility doesn't play a direct role in why you are experiencing stress, it plays a role in how you react to it. You may experience stress as the result of trauma, injury, disease or loss—things you cannot control. You are, however, still responsible for how you react to such circumstances and for the choices you make about how to cope. What you tell yourself *can* make a difference. Research has shown that people with serious spinal cord injuries fare better when they have an attitude of hope. An attitude of optimism has been connected with long-term survival in people with heart disease and cancer. A sense of control has been shown to affect longevity and well-being. And self-efficacy (the belief that you can achieve a specific goal or master a challenge) has been shown to decrease symptoms of depression and pain and increase immune functioning.

There is also evidence to support the positive effects on long-term health of believing one's life has meaning. Researchers have theorized that a sense of coherence, which includes finding meaning, was strongly related to survival among those who experienced the severe trauma of Nazi concentration camps.

This is not to say that you will negatively affect your health if you respond in a natural way to life events. You don't have to ignore feelings of anger, frustration, grief and bereavement that are often appropriate responses to life circumstances. The key is, once you have allowed yourself to feel these feelings and to work through them, to use your own personal power and resources to make the most of the circumstances you find yourself in.

Taking responsibility to educate yourself about stress provides you with a strong foundation for committing yourself to managing stress more effectively. Many of us are reluctant to take on this responsibility because we are afraid to fail. We instinctively know that guilt might follow failure and we anticipate emotionally beating ourselves up. Such commonly held fears are often part of negative, unhealthy programming from the past. Another reason many of us are reluctant to take responsibility for ourselves is that we have lost touch with ourselves. We no longer experience or trust the intuition we were born with that tells us what is right for us. We also may have lost touch with our physical body signals, not to mention our gut-level responses. Rather than turn inside to find the answers, we look outside ourselves to others.

In *High Level Wellness,* Donald Ardell says that "the single greatest cause of unhealth in this nation is that most Americans neglect, and surrender to others, responsibility for their own health." The sad truth is that many of us would rather take a pill than change our beliefs and behaviors. The current medical model seems to have a singular focus on existing pathology and symptoms and adheres to specialization and drugs as primary methods of treatment. This often serves to reinforce our sense of helplessness and lack of motivation to participate in our own healing. Even some forms of psychotherapy, such as psychoanalysis, do not support self-responsibility because the treatment model focuses principally on the past and the present rather than the future. Medical and mental health professionals who do not believe that their clients can change may also undermine the process of self-responsibility.

Self-responsibility does not mean rejecting traditional medical treatment. It does mean participating as fully as possible in your own health and well-being. It means accepting your stress symptoms. It also means learning to read your mind/body signals and to view them as important messages telling you what may be out of balance in your life.

Only when you accept responsibility for yourself can you develop the necessary awareness to identify your unique stressors. Then you can understand how you create your own stress. Self-responsibility in this book or elsewhere should not be construed as a "should" or a "must" or even a trigger for personal blame. This will only lead to more stress. Healthy self-responsibility, on the other hand, is an opportunity to participate in your own health and well-being to the fullest extent possible. Most importantly, it offers you the opportunity to use your personal power to take action, accepting that you have the capabilities and resources to respond to potential stressors in different, healthier ways. Once and for all, you may finally release the lock on old programming and be open to living your life with more health and inner peace.

Remember, *If you always do what you've always done, you'll always get what you've always gotten.*

Start today to do something different.

Success Stories

Many of my clients experience physical symptoms as a result of their reactions to a wide variety of stressors ranging from multiple combinations of dysfunctional and alcohol/substance abuse family issues to relationship and life change issues to career and money issues. They have presented with physical symptoms such as migraines, TMJ, chronic fatigue syndrome, fibromyalgia, cardiac problems, cancer, brain tumors, anxiety attacks, phobias, backaches, gastrointestinal problems, irritable bowel syndrome, and food and substance addictions. After clients have had their physical symptoms checked out by their health care provider, we identify and evaluate the various stressors which may be contributing to their symptoms. Then, we focus on a combination of strategies suitable to their needs.

I have a deep sense of honor and respect for my clients as complex, multidimensional, spiritual beings. It would take many more pages than this book allows to capture their uniqueness and individual learning process. With this in mind, the following descriptions are offered as brief vignettes to illustrate how my approach can be effective. I have changed names and some details in an effort to protect my clients' privacy. The first three cases are described more fully in Chapter 7.

Ellen

We first worked with Ellen's negative, distorted thinking concerning her work ("I could be laid off at any time and I wouldn't be able to cope with the loss of money and health benefits. . . . If only I could work harder and get this place running more efficiently we wouldn't have to lay off any more people"), assumptions she was making about what other people were thinking ("The employees blame me when there are layoffs"), and limiting beliefs and "shoulds" concerning getting her needs met ("I cannot waste time doing things for myself because my husband's and child's needs are more important"). Ellen began using breath work and meditation right away. Her nutrition and exercise regimens were already in line with lowering stress.

Working with emotions and getting needs met took some time due to the emotional, physical and sexual abuse Ellen had experienced as a child. Because of her abuse issues, Ellen found it extremely difficult to believe that she was worthy and deserving of happiness. This is where the spiritual strategies of loving detachment, self-acceptance, living in the present moment and nurturing her inner voice were particularly effective.

Ellen was very committed to making healthy changes in her life. Within four weeks her symptoms of sleeplessness, racing thoughts, grinding teeth, anxiety, gastrointestinal problems and inability to concentrate began to improve and she was thinking more positively. Over the course of several months she began to experiment with getting her needs met. She found appropriate caretakers for her handicapped son so she and her husband could have some quality time and enjoyment together; she rearranged and redefined her responsibilities at work; and, she took more time for herself.

Eventually, we worked on life planning issues and considering other possible job options. Because Ellen learned to expand her ideas of what was possible for her and because she had practiced getting her needs met, she was able to explore work opportunities that were more suited to her personal desires and capabilities. Ellen now has a new and very fulfilling job as a foster mother and advocate for mentally handicapped children. She is able to work in her home and be near her son, both of which are very important to her.

John

John began doing healing breath work, meditating, walking for exercise and eliminating caffeine from his diet right away. Then we worked on John's negative and distorted thinking regarding work and looked specifically at how these thoughts were threatening to him and causing his physical symptoms.

This involved identifying ways in which he was blowing things out of proportion ("If I don't get all this work done, I'll either be fired or I'll be personally responsible for slowing production") and assuming what other people were thinking ("The other workers are purposely bringing me bad film because they don't like me"). We also looked at thoughts and feelings around getting his needs met ("I don't have the right to take time off with all this work to be done") and his limiting beliefs or "shoulds" ("I should do the work on the house addition because I am capable, and because we'll save money").

After six weeks of our working together, John requested and received a one-week vacation which he took with his wife. By the end of two-and-a-half months, John was no longer experiencing racing and negative thoughts or shortness of breath. The periods of anxiety and heart palpitations had significantly decreased from several times a day to once every two weeks or so. Most important, John had learned how to become aware of moments of anxiety as they occurred and felt confident in his ability to control them and eliminate them quickly.

Marie

Although healing breath work, meditation, exercise and nutrition strategies were discussed with Marie several times, it took her several months to commit to making them a part of her lifestyle.

We began by examining how her thoughts were creating the experience of stress for her. She minimized her capabilities and contributions to the family ("Since I don't have a job and I am just a homemaker, I should be able to take care of the house, the kids, my husband and volunteer work with no problem") and relied on external rather than internal validation ("I am embarrassed to tell people that I am just a homemaker because they will think less of me," "My ex-husband will do anything to make my life miserable"). Marie also used "shoulds" and childhood programming as a means of not feeling worthy and deserving of happiness ("I don't deserve to take time for myself or with my husband if the house isn't taken care of." "I don't deserve to feel depressed. I have everything anyone could want").

We focused on strategies such as distorted thinking, eliminating negative self-talk, working with emotions, getting needs met, volunteering, seeing options, loving detachment, self-acceptance, self-compassion and nurturing her inner voice. She practiced getting her needs met and using loving detachment to get her husband and children to help out with chores so she could have more time for herself.

She also used the inner voice strategy and began to feel more internally validated. She used her sense of internal validation and detachment strategies as well as affirmations and positive self-talk to deal more effectively with her ex-husband. Marie's volunteer work at her church allowed her to feel greater self-esteem and self-worth. It also allowed her to practice getting her needs met as she learned to set limits for herself with some difficult people also involved in volunteering.

Within several months, Marie felt less tired, was not sick as often and was not experiencing anxiety. Although it took several more months, Marie's depressed feelings began to lift once she made a commitment to stick with the program, recognizing that she had options and practicing self-acceptance and self-compassion. In learning that she could change the way she perceived the stressors in her life, by looking for opportunities to get her needs met, and accepting and loving herself as she was, Marie became more optimistic and hopeful.

Janice

Janice began seeing me after being hospitalized the previous year for congestive heart failure and cardiomyopathy and more recently for unstable angina. After her first hospitalization she began to explore her options for participating in her own recovery and began following Dean Ornish's nutrition plan for cardiac patients which is essentially a whole foods diet which limits fat intake to 10 percent. In addition to nutrition, she was also either walking or using an exercise bike three times a week.

Janice was facing tremendous stress including a rocky second marriage, having to return to a high-pressure job for financial reasons, behavior problems with her two children, and the fear of dying from her condition. The adult child of an alcoholic mentally ill mother, Janice believed strongly in her unworthiness and undeservability as a human being. Her coping mechanism was to be codependent, i.e., to never stop doing for others long enough to examine her own needs and feelings.

Janice used strategies such as nutrition, exercise, daily meditation geared toward lowering stress and cholesterol, visualizations to reinforce healthy heart functioning, identifying needs and feelings, exploring origins of unworthiness and undeservability, and cognitive restructuring to overcome limiting beliefs. During the course of our work together, Janice has used all the strategies presented in this manual.

Within one month of making these strategies a part of her life along with psychotherapy, Janice was experiencing less stress overall, her coping skills on the job had markedly improved and her cholesterol had lowered significantly. After six months, Janice's unstable angina was under control and after nine months her doctor said that she had experienced "spontaneous recovery" from cardiomyopathy.

Her progress in reducing stress on the job came as a direct result of learning to view her work and her job in less threatening ways, asking for help when she needed it, using breathing and meditation daily, and effectively detaching both from issues that were not her responsibility and from difficult people. She also made great progress in understanding how her childhood programming affected her present feelings and behaviors as well as reprogramming her sense of worthiness and deservability. She continues to work on finding meaning through life planning and stress hardiness strategies and developing a more loving relationship with herself and others through self-acceptance, self-compassion and effective communication strategies.

Sue

Sue experienced three to four day-long migraines on a monthly, and sometimes weekly, basis since the age of 12. Doctors had all concentrated on various neurological and physiological explanations and offered drug therapy. We worked on a program involving meditation and relaxation as well as identifying stressors that might lead to a migraine. We quickly learned that, for a variety reasons, Sue experienced migraines within 24 hours of seeing or sometimes talking on the phone with her mother and her ex-husband.

With this knowledge we worked on the thoughts and beliefs Sue had developed which caused her to view her mother and ex-husband as threatening to her. Within several weeks Sue was able to change her thoughts and beliefs about both these people. By exploring her emotions and needs regarding her mother and ex-husband she was also better prepared for her contact with them.

Through positive self-talk, establishing healthy limits and boundaries and getting her needs met, Sue was also able to significantly lower the stress she experienced around these two people. With the help of relaxation and meditation strategies, Sue was able to recognize when her body was getting tense and take steps to release the tension. After using the above strategies her migraines were significantly reduced in number and duration.

Sue has since weaned herself off all seven medications she was taking for headaches and now uses only relaxation, meditation and positive self-talk to manage headache pain, which occurs only rarely.

Ann

Ann presented with an 18-year history of intermittent anxiety attacks while driving. At the time she came to see me she was drinking two glasses of wine in the morning to overcome her fear before driving to school, where she was completing an undergraduate degree. In addition, she had been taking the antianxiety drug Klonopin for at least five years. She had been in counseling previously for several years.

Besides the anxiety attacks while driving, stressors for Ann included a demanding schedule of school, work and social activities; career concerns; expectations from her parents; communication issues with her husband and evaluating whether to have children as her 40th birthday approached. Together, we developed a program which included meditation, visualization, time management, no drinking before driving, understanding the stress response, positive self-talk and affirmations, evaluating and eliminating "shoulds," exploring and implementing ways to get her needs met, nutrition and exercise.

We were able to connect her anxiety attacks with an underlying fear of asserting her needs and her individuality. During each period in her life when she found herself pursuing goals that were different from her mother's, Ann would experience anxiety attacks. Ann's mother was a traditional housewife with strong beliefs about women's roles such as, "Women should be wives and mothers first," and "Women should subjugate their needs to the needs of others."

Within two weeks of using the previously mentioned strategies Ann ceased having anxiety attacks. I believe that the critical factors in Ann's case included high motivation, commitment to and follow-through on strategies and making the introspective, emotional connection concerning her symptoms. Previous counseling also helped us to cut through to core issues quickly.

Grace

Grace came to see me six weeks after being diagnosed with stage 5 cervical cancer. She had just undergone an emergency partial hysterectomy and was scheduled for a series of eight radiation treatments to fight the remaining cancer. No stranger to doctors and invasive medical procedures, Grace had also been battling painful endometriosis for the past five years. At the age of 32, Grace worked 60 to 70 hours a week as a lawyer, work that she didn't find satisfying. As a newlywed, married to a corporate executive, she was deeply shaken by the probability that the partial hysterectomy and continued endometriosis would interfere with her dream of having children.

Luckily, Grace was very focused and willing to participate in her own healing. She had already done a great deal of research, had begun a macrobiotic diet and was open to working on the emotional components of her illness. In taking control, committing to healing herself and seeing her illness as an opportunity to make healthy changes in her life, Grace was already exhibiting the attributes of being stress hardy.

In the first few sessions, we learned that Grace engaged in a great deal of negative self-talk and "shoulds." Because of childhood programming, she told herself things like, "I should look, act and dress perfectly all the time. I should be in control of myself and everything that happens to me at all times. It's not okay to show emotion. Whatever I do is never good enough. I'm not good enough. It's not okay for a woman to be strong and athletic. It's more important to make money than to do something you love to do."

Because she believed that she wasn't good enough and that she should be perfect, Grace found that she overprepared for many things in her daily life—work, cooking, housecleaning and even dressing. She found it difficult to just be herself. In fact, it was hard for her to know just who she was. All through high school she had enjoyed art and woodworking projects and had even won some awards for her work. Her parents, however, disapproved of Grace's desire to major in art in college or to pursue this kind of work as a career. Instead, they pressured her to go on to law school after graduation. As a people-pleaser, Grace learned early on to suppress her own wants and needs in order to satisfy others.

We began immediately with a program of daily meditation and guided imagery, as well as exercise, changing negative self-talk and shoulds. Eager to develop self-awareness and to make positive changes, Grace quickly absorbed other strategies such as recognizing distorted thinking, self-love, self-acceptance, self-compassion, inner voice work and gratitude.

After completing four of the recommended eight radiation treatments, Grace was told she was free of cancer. We don't know which of the components of Grace's program worked together to overcome the cancer. Was it just the radiation treatment or did a macrobiotic diet, an optimistic and hopeful attitude, supportive counseling and stress-relieving strategies also play a role? The science of PNI is getting closer and closer to giving us these answers. In the meantime, people like Grace can feel empowered by participating in their own emotional and physical healing process.

But there's more to this story. Learning that she was cancer-free did not stop Grace from continuing to learn more about herself, her emotions and her needs. She still faced going back to a job and a profession she didn't enjoy, as well as dealing with motherhood and fertility issues.

While we used all of the strategies described in this book, three strategies were particularly important at this juncture.

Grace used inner voice work and the self-reflection tool in order to identify what she was thinking, feeling and needing. She also used the life-planning exercise to explore who she was and how she wanted to live out her new lease on life. She went on to reduce her work load to part-time and to set limits with aggressive co-workers in an atmosphere where personal needs were not honored.

Over the next year, Grace committed to taking more time for herself, for her art and woodworking and for having more fun. She experimented with letting go of her rigidity around over-preparing and housecleaning, and she even tried a new, more relaxed style of dressing. Motherhood continued to be an issue, but Grace used her ability for self-reflection and emotional awareness to nurture herself and continue to explore her options.

Our time together ended after a year or so when Grace and her husband decided to quit their jobs and their careers and move to Vermont in pursuit of more meaningful work and more satisfying lifestyles.

Sam

I met Sam right after his 81st birthday. In the last 10 years since his retirement, Sam had had a heart attack and seven operations including surgical procedures for a hernia, cataracts, heart bypass and valve replacement and gall bladder removal. During this time he was also treated for depression with a variety of medications, day hospital programs, and most recently with electric shock treatments. For the past year, Sam had been experiencing panic attacks, generalized anxiety and depressed moods.

His daily routine was to wake up at 9:00 a.m., nauseous and anxious, eat breakfast, take a Xanax (antianxiety medication) and return to bed at 10:00 a.m. Around 4:00 p.m., he would begin to feel well enough to get up and eat dinner. Several hours later, he returned to bed for the night. He experienced panic attacks every day, especially when he thought about having to go anywhere.

Before retiring, Sam was a vibrant, energetic business owner. Over the last 10 years he had given up all activities except reading, and that was difficult because his eyesight was failing. He and his second wife of 28 years, Martha, had just moved into a planned community for senior citizens and had been looking forward to meeting new people, participating in social events and activities and traveling. There was tension between the couple because Sam's illnesses and depressed moods kept them from doing these things and enjoying each other. Sam felt guilty for holding Martha back and Martha was frustrated and disappointed with Sam's physical and emotional health.

Because Sam lived two hours away, I made several "house calls" in order to see him and followed up between visits with phone calls. On my first visit I asked him to rank his mood on an average day over the last year on a scale from one to ten, with ten being a great day. Sam answered that his days were a four or five.

Then we centered on issues of low self-esteem, guilt, "shoulds" and negative thinking. Sam was very critical of himself because of his emotional and physical condition. Sam's anxiety seemed to be connected to feelings of not being safe, not feeling lovable, not accomplishing anything and feeling powerless over what was happening to him. We did a guided imagery exercise that focused on finding a safe place and connecting with feelings of personal power, motivation and finding options.

In addition to working with "shoulds," guilt, negative thinking, and seeing options, Sam began to use the Daily Program I recommend to each of my clients (see page 93). For Sam, this meant doing the Peaceful Wake-Up Call each morning with a particular focus on the gratitude part of the exercise, as well as deep breathing every hour for three minutes, using affirmations we developed together, listening to a meditation/relaxation tape in the morning and late afternoon, and finishing the day with the same steps in the Peaceful Wake-Up Call.

Some of his affirmations included: "I'm creating everything I need for my health and happiness. I'm moving through my day easily and effortlessly. I am safe. I am loved." We made a list of all the things that Sam could do when he felt anxious, such as various forms of active meditation like counting his steps as he walked, listening to a relaxation tape, watching a comedy on TV or VCR or the wonder exercise (see page 158).

His job between our visits was to lengthen this list of activities to curb anxiety and to consider committing to an exercise program, seeing a nutritionist, volunteering, exploring hobbies and hiring a companion/driver. Sam also agreed to try to stay up all day rather than returning to bed after breakfast.

Over the next several weeks, Sam worked diligently on the Daily Program, stayed out of bed and experienced a significant decrease in panic attacks and general anxiety. The frequency of his panic attacks decreased from several a day to several a week and tapered off completely within three weeks. Around this time, he began seeing a local psychotherapist on a weekly basis. He found these meetings to be very supportive and helpful. Sam also found a driver/companion that he really connected with and whose company he enjoyed a great deal. Although he was feeling better, Sam resisted volunteering, socializing or finding hobbies.

On our next visit together we used guided imagery to connect Sam with feelings of being a good person, satisfaction in having helped others, personal power in surviving several emotional traumas, and humor about growing old. We used these feelings as inspiration for the Self-Acceptance, Self-Compassion and Self-Love strategies. Sam, Martha and I also worked on Identifying Your Needs and Effective Communication Skills.

After six weeks Sam was not experiencing anxiety in the morning at all and reported that as long as he had a plan for the day he felt good. He exercised regularly, saw a nutritionist, read large-print books and signed up for classes at the local community learning center. He also found that when he was busy he forgot to take Xanax and that he felt better without it. He consistently ranked his mood as an eight, nine and sometimes even a ten.

Sam's spirits continued to rise with his level of community involvement and connection with other people. Over the next eight to ten months, he kept up with his previous routine and got involved in some committees and volunteer work where he lived. Even though Sam still worried about being away from home for longer than several hours, he didn't let it hold him back. He and Martha socialized a great deal more, attended plays and concerts, and traveled. Sam's local psychotherapist continued to be instrumental in supporting and encouraging him.

As I write this, Sam is dying of old age; some of his organs are just not functioning anymore. His spirits are good, he accepts his condition, feels loved and cared for, and asks for what he needs, like spending time with family. For now, he is only mildly uncomfortable and sleeps most of the day.

As with all of my clients, I feel both graced and grateful for the opportunity to be part of Sam's life journey. I feel a particular sense of awe over the way Sam turned his life around and healed himself emotionally and physically in the last 19 months. I'm happy that his passing will be peaceful for him and those who love him. His memory will always bring a sparkle to my eyes and a light to my heart.

Appendix

Chapter Notes

Chapters 1 and 2

Benson, H. (1996). *Timeless Healing*. NY: Scribner.

Borysenko, J. (1987). *Minding the Body, Mending the Mind*. NY: Bantam Books.

Breggin, P. (1994). *Talking Back to Prozac*. NY: St. Martin's Press.

Breggin, P. (1991). *Toxic Psychiatry*. NY: St. Martin's Press.

Burton, T. & Ono, Y. Campaign for Prozac Targets Consumers. *Wall Street Journal*. (1997, July 1).

Chopra, D. (1989). *Quantum Healing*. NY: Bantam Books.

Colbert, T. (1996). *Broken Brains or Wounded Hearts*. CA: Kevco Publishing.

Critser, G. (June, 1996). Oh, how happy we will be. *Harper's Magazine*.

Davison, G. & Neale, J. (1982). *Abnormal psychology: An experimental clinical approach*. NY: Wiley.

Dienstfrey, H. (1991). *Where the Mind Meets the Body*. NY: HarperCollins.

Everly, G., & Rosenfeld, R. (1981). *The Nature and Treatment of the Stress Response*. NY: Plenum Press.

Girdano, D., Everly, G., Dusek, D. (1990). *Controlling Stress and Tension*. NJ: Prentice Hall.

Healthy people 2000: National health promotion and disease prevention objectives. (1990). *Department of Health and Human Services*. U.S. Publication No. (PHS) 91–50213.

Hunt, M. (1987). Therapies: A brief history. *New York Times Magazine*. August 30, pp. 28–30.

Kramer, P. (1993). *Listening to Prozac*. NY: Viking Press.

Lilly Sales Rise As Use of Prozac Keeps Growing. *Wall Stroeet Journal*. (1996, January 31).

Nicholi, A. (Ed.). (1988). *The New Harvard Guide to Psychiatry*. MA: Harvard University Press.

Ornstein, R., & Sobel, D. (1987). *The Healing Brain*. NY: Simon and Schuster.

Pelletier, K. (1977). *Mind as Healer, Mind as Slayer*. NY: Dell.

Pelletier, K. (1993). Between mind and body: Stress, emotions, and health. In D. Goleman & J. Gurin (Eds.). *Mind/Body Medicine*. (pp. 19–38). NY: Consumer Reports Books.

Prozac: The wonder drug. *Providence Sunday Journal*. UPI Wire Service. (1993, November 21). Section B, pp. 1.

Toffler, A. (1970). *Future Shock*. NY: Bantam Books.

Toffler, A. (1980). *The Third Wave*. NY: Bantam Books.

Chapter 3

Appley, M., & Trumbell, R. (Eds.). (1986). *Dynamics of Stress*. NY: Plenum Press.

Chalmers, B.E. (1981). A selective review of stress: Some cognitive approaches taken a step further. *Current Psychological Reviews*, 1. pp. 325–344.

Dienstfrey, H. (1991). *Where the Mind Meets the Body*. NY: HarperCollins.

Ellis, A. (1973). *Humanistic Psychology: The Rational-Emotive Approach*. NY: Julian Publishers.

Everly, G., & Rosenfeld, R. (1981). *The Nature and Treatment of the Stress Response*. NY: Plenum Press.

Goldberger, L., & Breznitz, S. (Eds.). (1982). *Handbook of Stress: Theoretical and Clinical Aspects*. NY: The Free Press.

Holmes, T., & Rahe, R. (1967). The social readjustment rating scale. *Journal of Psychosomatic Research*, 11. pp. 213–218.

Lazarus, R. (1966). *Psychological Stress and the Coping Process*. NY: McGraw Hill.

Mikhail, A. (1981). Stress: A psychophysiological conception. *Journal of Human Stress*, 7. pp. 9–15.

Monat, A., & Lazarus, R. (Eds.). (1985). *Stress and Coping*. NY: Columbia University Press.

Ornstein, R., & Sobel, D. (1987). *The Healing Brain*. NY: Simon and Schuster.

Pert, C. (1986). The wisdom of the receptors. *Advances*, vol. 3, no. 3.

Selye, H. (1974). *Stress without Distress*. Philadelphia: Lippincott.

Chapter 4

Barefoot, J. In: Williams, R. (1989). *The Trusting Heart*. (pp. 44–71). NY: Times Books.

Bartrop, R., Lazarus, L., & Luckhurst, E. (1977). Depressed lymphocyte function after bereavement. *Lancet, 1*. pp. 834–839.

Cohen, D., Tyrell, A., & Smith, A. (1991). Psychological stress and susceptibility to the common cold. *New England Journal of Medicine, 325*. pp. 606–612.

Dembrowski, T., Macdougall, J., Eliot, R. & Buell, J. (1984). Moving beyond Type A. *Advances, 1*. pp. 16–26.

Friedman, M. (1984). *Treating Type-A Behavior and Your Heart*. NY: Ballantine Books.

House, J., Landis, K. & Umberson, D. (1988). Social relationships and health. *Science, 241*. pp. 540–545.

Kasel, V., Evans, A., & Niederman, J. (1979). Psychosocial risk factors in the development of mononucleosis. *Psychosomatic Medicine, 41*. pp. 445–466.

Kemeny, M., Cohen, F. & Zegans, L. (1989). Psychological and immunological predictors of genital herpes recurrence. *Psychosomatic Medicine, 51*. pp. 195–208.

Kiecolt-Glaser, J., & Glaser, R. (1993). Mind and immunity. In D. Goleman & J. Gurin (Eds.). *Mind/Body Medicine*. (pp. 39–64). NY: Consumer Reports Books.

Kiecolt-Glaser, J., & Glaser, R. (1985). Psychosocial enhancement of immunocompetence in a geriatric population. *Health Psychology, 4*. pp. 25–41.

Kiecolt-Glaser, J., Garner, W., Speicher, E., Penn, G, and Glaser, R. (1984). Psychosocial modifiers of immunocompetence in medical students. *Psychosomatic Medicine, 46*. pp. 7–14.

Locke, S., Kraus, J., & Lesserman, J. (1984). Life-change stress, psychiatric symptoms and natural killer cell activity. *Psychosomatic Medicine, 46*. pp. 441–453.

Poole, William. (1993). *The Heart of Healing*. Atlanta: Turner Publishing.

Schleifer, S., Keller, S., & Cammerino, M. (1983). Suppression of lymphocyte stimulation following bereavement. *Journal of the American Medical Association, 250.* pp. 374–377.

Shekelle, R.B., Gale, M., Ostfeld, A.M. & Paul, O. (1983). Hostility, risk of coronary heart disease and mortality. *Psychosomatic Medicine, 45.* pp. 109–114.

Williams, R.B., Haney, T.L. & Lee, K.L. (1980). Type-A behavior, hostility and coronary atherosclerosis. *Psychosomatic Medicine, 42.* pp. 539–549.

Chapter 5

Antoni, M., Baggett, L., Ironson, G., LaPerriere, A., August, S., & Klimas, N. (1991). Cognitive-behavioral stress management intervention buffers distress responses and immunologic changes following notification of HIV-1 seropositivity. *Journal of Clinical and Consulting Psychology, 59.* pp. 909–915.

Antonovsky, A. (1987). *Unravelling the Mystery of Health: How People Manage Stress and Stay Well.* San Francisco: Jossey-Bass.

Borysenko, J. (1985). Healing motives: An interview with David McClelland. *Advances, 2.* pp. 35–36.

Borysenko, J. (1987). *Minding the Body, Mending the Mind.* NY: Bantam Books.

Byrd, R. (1988). Positive therapeutic effects of intercessory prayer in a coronary care unit population. *Southern Medical Journal, 81.* pp. 826–829.

Derogatis, L., Abeloff, M. & Melisaratos, N. (1979). Psychological coping mechanisms and survival time in metastatic breast cancer. *Journal of the American Medical Association, 242.* pp. 1504–1508.

Frankl, V. (1984). *Man's Search for Meaning.* NY: Pocket Books.

Girdano, D., Everly, G., Dusek, D. (1990). *Controlling Stress and Tension.* NJ: Prentice Hall.

Glaser, R., Kiecolt-Glaser, J., & Speicher, C. (1985). Stress, loneliness, and changes in herpes virus latency. *Journal of Behavioral Medicine, 8.* pp. 249–260.

Greer, S., & Morris, T. (1975). Psychological attributes of women who develop breast cancer. *Psychosomatic Research, 19.* pp. 147–153.

Holman, H., & Lorig, K. (1992). Perceived self-efficacy in self-management of chronic disease. In R. Schwarzer (Ed.). *Self-efficacy: Thought Control of Action.* NY: Hemisphere Publications.

Kabat-Zinn, J. (1990). *Full Catastrophe Living.* NY: Delacorte Press.

Kobasa, S. (1979). Stressful life events, personality, and health: An inquiry into hardiness. *Journal of Personality and Social Psychology, 37.* pp 1–11.

Kobasa, S., Maddi, S., & Kahn, S. (1982). Hardiness and health: A prospective study. *Journal of Personality and Social Psychology, 42.* pp. 169–170.

Langer, E., & Rodin, J. (1977). Long-term effects of a control-relevant intervention with the institutionalized aged. *Journal of Personality and Social Psychology, 35.* pp. 897–902.

Ornish, D. (1990). *Reversing Heart Disease.* NY: Ballantine Books.

Ornish, D., Gotto, A., & Miller, R. (1979). Effects of vegetarian diet and selected yoga techniques in the treatment of coronary heart disease. *Clinical Research, 27.* pp. 720–732.

Peterson, C., & Bossio, L. (1993). Healthy attitudes: Optimism, hope and control. In D. Goleman & J. Gurin (Eds.). *Mind/Body Medicine.* (pp. 351–366). NY: Consumer Reports Books.

Peterson, C., Seligman, M., & Vaillant, G. (1988). Explanatory style as a risk factor for physical illness: A thirty-five year longitudinal study. *Journal of Personality and Social Psychology, 55.* pp. 23–28.

Schmale, A., & Iker, H. (1971). Hopelessness as a predictor of cervical cancer. *Social Science and Medicine, 5.* pp. 95–100.

Seligman, M. (1975). *Learned Helplessness.* San Francisco: W.H. Freeman & Co.

Seligman, M. (1990). *Learned Optimism.* NY: Pocket Books.

Speigel, D., Bloom, J., Kraemer, H. & Gottheil, E. (1989). Effect of psychosocial treatment on survival of patients with metastatic breast cancer. *Lancet.* pp. 888–891.

Temoshok, L. & Knier, A. In J. Holland & S. Lewis. Emotions and cancer: what do we really know? D. Goleman & J. Gurin (Eds.). *Mind/Body Medicine.* (pp. 85–109). NY: Consumer Reports Books.

Thomas, C. (1988). Cancer and the youthful mind: A forty-year perspective. *Advances, 5.* pp. 42–58.

Wallis, C. (1993, November 4). Why new age medicine is catching on. *Time Magazine.* pp. 68–76.

Chapter 6

Antoni, M., Baggett, L., Ironson, G., La Perriere, A., August, S., & Klimas, N. (1991). Cognitive-behavioral stress management intervention buffers distress responses and immunologic changes following notification of HIV-1 seropositivity. *Journal of Clinical and Consulting Psychology, 59.* pp. 909–915.

Beck, A. & Rush, A. (1978). Cognitive approaches to depression and suicide. In G. Servan (Ed.). *Cognitive Defects in the Development of Mental Illness.* (pp. 235–257). NY: Brunner Mazel.

Beck, A., Emery, G., & Greenberg, R. (1985). *Anxiety and Phobias: A Cognitive Approach.* NY: Basic Books.

Benson, H. (1975). *The Relaxation Response.* NY: Morrow.

Burns, D. (1989). *Feeling Good Handbook.* NY: Plume Co.

Holman, H., & Lorig, K. (1992). Perceived self-efficacy in self-management of chronic disease. In R. Schwarzer (Ed.). *Self-efficacy: Thought Control of Action.* NY: Hemisphere Publications.

Kiecolt-Glaser, J., & R. Glaser. (1985). Psychosocial enhancement of immunocompetence in a geriatric population. *Health Psychology, 4.* pp. 25–41.

Kabat-Zinn, J., Lipworth, L., Burney, R., & Sellers, W. (1986). Four-year follow-up of a meditation-based program for the self-regulation of chronic pain: Treatment outcomes and compliance. *The Journal of Pain, 2.* (3), pp. 159–173.

Ornish, D. (1990). *Reversing Heart Disease.* NY: Ballantine Books.

Ornish, D., Gotto, A., & Miller, R. (1979). Effects of vegetarian diet and selected yoga techniques in the treatment of coronary heart disease. *Clinical Research, 27.* pp. 720–732.

Pennebaker, J., Kiecolt-Glaser, J., & Glaser, R. (1988). Disclosure of traumas and immune function: Health implications for psychotherapy. *Journal of Consulting and Clinical Psychology, 56.* pp. 239–245.

Rush, A., Beck, A., Kovacs, M., & Hollon, S. (1977). Comparative efficacy of cognitive therapy and pharmacotherapy in the treatment of depressed outpatients. *Cognitive Therapy and Research, 1.* pp. 17–37.

Simonton, C., Matthews-Simonton, S., & Creighton, J. (1978). *Getting Well Again.* NY: Bantam Books.

Speigel, D., Bloom, J., Kraemer, H. & Gottheil, E. (1989). Effect of psychosocial treatment on survival of patients with metastatic breast cancer. *Lancet.* pp. 888–891.

Widenfeld, S., O'Leary, A., & Bandura, A. (1990). Impact of self-efficacy in coping with stressors on components of the immune system. *Journal of Personality and Social Psychology, 59.* pp. 1082–1094.

Chapter 7

Appley, M., & Trumbell, R. (Eds.). (1986). *Dynamics of Stress.* NY: Plenum Press.

Everly, G., & Rosenfeld, R. (1981). *The Nature and Treatment of the Stress Response.* NY: Plenum Press.

Girdano, D., Everly, G., Dusek, D. (1990). *Controlling Stress and Tension*. NJ: Prentice Hall.

Goldberger, L., & Breznitz, S. (Eds.). (1982). *Handbook of Stress: Theoretical and Clinical Aspects*. NY: The Free Press.

Goliszek, A. (1992). *60 Second Stress Management*. NJ: Far Horizon Press.

Kabat-Zinn, J. (1990). *Full Catastrophe Living*. NY: Delacorte Press.

Margolis, C. & Shrier, L. (1982). *Manual of Stress Management*. PA: Franklin Institute.

Miller, L. & Smith, A.D. (1993). *The Stress Solution*. NY: Pocket Books.

Pelletier, K. (1993). Between mind and body: Stress, emotions, and health. In D. Goleman & J. Gurin (Eds.). *Mind/Body Medicine*. (pp. 19–38). NY: Consumer Reports Books.

Shaffer, M. (1982). *Life after Stress*. NY: Plenum Press.

Chapter 9

Bandler, R. (1987). *Using Your Brain for a Change*. Utah: Real People Press.

Bandler, R., & Grinder, J. (1979). *Frogs into Princes: Neuro-Linguistic Programming*. Utah: Real People Press.

Beattie, M. (1989) *Beyond Codependency*. San Francisco: Harper & Row Publishers.

Beck, A. & Rush, A. (1978). Cognitive approaches to depression and suicide. In G. Servan (Ed.). *Cognitive Defects in the Development of Mental Illness*. (pp. 235–257). NY: Brunner Mazel.

Beck, A., Emery, G., & Greenberg, R. (1985). *Anxiety and Phobias: A Cognitive Approach*. NY: Basic Books.

Benson, H., & Stuart, E. (1992). *The Wellness Book*. NY: Fireside.

Bradshaw, J. (1988). *The Family*. FL: Health Communications.

Branden, N. (1983). *Honoring the Self*. NY: Bantam Books.

Burns, D. (1989). *Feeling Good Handbook*. NY: Plume Co.

Capra, F. (1975). *The Tao of Physics*. CA: Shambala.

Chopra, D. (1989). *Quantum Healing*. NY: Bantam Books.

Coit, L. (1992). *Listening: How to Increase Awareness of Your Inner Guide*. CA: Las Brisas Retreat.

Ellis, A. (1973). *Humanistic Psychology: The Rational-Emotive Approach*. NY: Julian Publishers.

Girdano, D., Everly, G., Dusek, D. (1990). *Controlling Stress and Tension*. NJ: Prentice Hall.

Kobasa, S. (1979). Stressful life events, personality, and health: An inquiry into hardiness. *Journal of Personality and Social Psychology,* *37.* pp. 1–11.

McKay, M., & Fanning, P. (1987). Self-Esteem. NY: St. Martin's Press.

Muller, W. (1992). *Legacy of the Heart.* NY: Fireside.

Reich, W. (1969). *Selected Writings.* NY: Farrar Publishing.

Saltoon, D. (1991). *The Common Book of Consciousness.* CA: Celestial Arts.

Siegel, B. (1986). *Love, Medicine and Miracles.* NY: Harper & Row.

Whitfield, C., (1987). *Healing the Child Within.* FL: Health Communications.

Travis, J., & Ryan, R. (1981). *Wellness Workbook.* CA: Ten Speed Press.

Zukav, G. (1979). *The Dancing Wu Li Masters.* NY: Bantam Books.

Chapter 10

Antonovsky, A. (1987). *Unravelling the Mystery of Health: How People Manage Stress and Stay Well.* San Francisco: Jossey-Bass.

Beattie, M. (1987). *Codependency No More.* San Francisco: Harper & Row Publishers.

Beck, A., Rush, A. Shaw, B. & Emery, G. (1979). *Cognitive Therapy of Depression.* NY: Guilford.

Bradshaw, J. (1989). *Healing the Shame that Binds You.* FL: Health Communications.

Burns, D. (1980). *Feeling Good: The New Mood Therapy.* NY: William Morrow & Co.

Brennan, C. (1994). The breath of well-being. *The Synthesis Newsletter.* Spring, pp. 1–2.

Carrington, P. (1977). *Freedom in Meditation.* NJ: Pace Educational Systems.

Covey. S. (1989). *Seven Habits of Highly Effective People.*

Frankl, V. (1984). *Man's Search for Meaning.* NY: Pocket Books.

Girdano, D., Everly, G., Dusek, D. (1990). *Controlling Stress and Tension.* NJ: Prentice Hall.

Hay, L. (1984). *You Can Heal your Life.* CA: Hay House.

Holman, H., & Lorig, K. (1992). Perceived self-efficacy in self-management of chronic disease. In R. Schwarzer (Ed.). *Self-efficacy: Thought Control of Action.* NY: Hemisphere Publications.

Horney, K. (1950). *Neurosis and Human Growth.* NY: W.W. Norton & Company.

House, J., Landis, K. & Umberson, D. (1988). Social relationships and health. *Science, 241.* pp. 540–545.

Kobasa, S. (1979). Stressful life events, personality, and health: An inquiry into hardiness. *Journal of Personality and Social Psychology,* 37. pp. 1–11.

Kobasa, S., Maddi, S., & Kahn, S. (1982). Hardiness and health: A prospective study. *Journal of Personality and Social Psychology,* 42. pp. 169–170.

Langer, E., & Rodin, J. (1977). Long-term effects of a control-relevant intervention with the institutionalized aged. *Journal of Personality and Social Psychology,* 35. pp. 897–902.

Lemerond, T. (1992). Laughter and humor. *Health Counselor,* 4, (4), pp. 28–29.

Luks, A. & Payne, P. (1992). *The Healing Power of Doing Good.* NY: Ballantine Books.

McKay, M., & Fanning, P. (1987). *Self-esteem.* NY: St. Martin's Press.

Miller, R. (1994, May/June). The breath of life. *Yoga Journal.* pp. 83–142.

Peterson, C., & Bossio, L. (1993). Healthy attitudes: Optimism, hope and control. In D. Goleman & J. Gurin (Eds.). *Mind/Body Medicine.* (pp. 351–366). NY: Consumer Reports Books.

Research Highlights. (1994). *Noetic Sciences Review, Fall.* CA: Institute for Noetic Sciences.

Rosen, R. (1994, March/April). Learning about the breath. *Yoga Journal.* p. 17.

Sacks, M. (1993). Exercise for stress control. In D. Goleman & J. Gurin (Eds.). *Mind/Body Medicine.* (pp. 315–328). NY: Consumer Reports Books.

Seligman, M. (1990). *Learned Optimism.* NY: Pocket Books.

Sharon, R. Assertive Bill of Rights. Originally appeared in Travis, J., & Ryan, R. (1981). *Wellness Workbook.* CA: Ten Speed Press.

Travis, J., & Ryan, R. (1981). *Wellness Workbook.* CA: Ten Speed Press.

Whitfield, C. (1987). *Healing the Child Within.* FL: Health Communications.

Widenfeld, S., O'Leary, A., & Bandura, A. (1990). Impact of self-efficacy in coping with stressors on components of the immune system. *Journal of Personality and Social Psychology,* 59. pp. 1082–1094.

Chapter 11

Handly, R., (1985). Anxiety and Panic Attacks: Their Cause and Cure. NY: Fawcett Crest.

Zuercher-White, Elke. (1995). An End to Panic. CA: New Harbinger Publications.

Tape and Workshop Information

Dr. Lori Leyden-Rubenstein has prepared a guided meditation tape to help you get started with several important stress management strategies described in *The Stress Management Handbook*. This 60 minute tape includes four guided meditations for breathing, autogenic stress relief, peaceful relaxation and listening to your inner voice.

Dr. Leyden-Rubenstein also conducts workshops and lectures based on this book as well as a variety of topics including:

Overcoming Anxiety/Panic Attacks Without Medication
Finding Your Soul Purpose
Living With Joy
Loving Yourself as a Spiritual Practice
Accessing Your Inner Strength & Wisdom

If you are ordering tapes or would like to be on her mailing list for workshops or lectures in your area, please send your name and address to:

Lori Leyden-Rubenstein
131 Sedgefield Rd
N. Kingstown, RI 02852
FAX: 401–294–3581

☐ Please put me on your mailing list.

☐ I have enclosed $ _____ to cover the cost of _____ tapes. When ordering tapes, please send check or money order for $10.00 plus $2.00 shipping & handling for each tape. (RI residents please add 7% sales tax.)

Index